A Work Behavior Analysis of Professional Counselors

Created by the National Board for Certified Counselors

Coordinated by

Larry C. Loesch, Ph.D., NCC
NBCC Evaluations Coordinator

Nicholas A. Vacc, EdD., NCC
NBCC Examination Consultant

Co-Published by

The National Board for Certified Counselors
3-D Terrace Way
Greensboro, NC 27403

Routledge
Taylor & Francis Group
LONDON AND NEW YORK

A Work Behavior Analysis of Professional Counselors

First published 1993 by Accelerated Development Inc. Publishers

Published 2020 by Routledge
2 Park Square, Milton Park, Abingdon, Oxon OX14 4RN
605 Third Avenue, New York, NY 10017

First issued in paperback 2021

Routledge is an imprint of the Taylor & Francis Group, an informa business

Publisher's Note
The publisher has gone to great lengths to ensure the quality of this reprint but points out that some imperfections in the original copies may be apparent.

Technical Development: Cynthia Long, Marguerite Mader, Janet Merchant, Shaeney Pigman, Sheila Sheward

Library of Congress Cataloging-in-Publication Data

A Work behavior analysis of professional counselors / created by the National Board for Certified Counselors ; coordinated by Larry C. Loesch, Nicholas A. Vacc.
p. cm.
Includes bibliographical references and index.
ISBN 1-55959-053-X
1. Counseling. 2. Task analysis. 3. Counselors--Certification.
I. Loesch, Larry C. II. Vacc, Nicholas A. III. National Board for Certified Counselors (U.S.)
BF637.C6W665 1993
361.3'23'023--dc20 93-27915
CIP

LCN: 93-27915

ISBN 13: 978-1-138-98732-6 (pbk)
ISBN 13: 978-1-55959-053-2 (hbk)
ISBN 13: 978-1-315-79277-4 (ebk)

DOI: 10.4324/9781315792774

ACKNOWLEDGEMENTS

The authors express their sincere and grateful appreciation to Mr. Chester Robinson, M.Ed., NCC, for his valuable assistance in conducting most of the data analyses for this study, and to Ms. Judy Garis, Ms. Candayce Spires, Ms. Donna Johnson, Ms. Sandra Ritter, and Ms. Victoria Wildermuth for their assistance in the preparation of the manuscript.

PREFACE

This study was conceived in the winter of 1984, in response to the profession's efforts to achieve counselor licensure. Licensure of counselors brought about the concern of what defines the practice of a professional counselor. The study had its origins in two sources: (a) the National Board for Certified Counselors' and staff members' functioning and (b) a commitment by NBCC to strengthen the credentialing of counselors and incur the expense to conduct a study of this magnitude.

Since its official inception in 1982, the National Board for Certified Counselors, Inc. (NBCC) has had as its primary purpose the provision of an effective professional counselor certification process, one that meets the highest professional standards. The fact that by late 1992 approximately 20,000 professional counselors had *voluntarily* sought and achieved the designation "National Certified Counselor" stands as testimony to NBCC's success in fulfilling this purpose. This success has been achieved in large part because of NBCC's continuing commitment to further development and refinement of its certification processes as well as the materials and resources (e.g., the National Counselor Examination) used within those processes.

A second, but certainly not secondary, NBCC purpose has been to facilitate activities that are of benefit to all who identify themselves as professional counselors. One of these activities is professional research. However, NBCC neither intends nor is able to support unsolicited research. Rather, it initiates research activities judged to be important in fulfilling its primary purpose *and* to have potential value across the broad spectrum of the counseling profession. It was within this perspective that the research described herein was conducted.

This book was developed to provide all practicing or aspiring counselors and interested others access to the results of the study. We have attempted (to the best of our ability) to make this book as comprehensible as possible. However, because of the nature of the study and the data sets derived from the research, many numbers and data analyses are included. Accordingly, even though we have reviewed the data presented several times, it is possible that some transcription errors may have occurred in the manuscript preparation. We accept all responsibility for the accuracy of the data presented.

Larry C. Loesch
Nicholas A. Vacc
1993

TABLE OF CONTENTS

LIST OF TABLES

Chapter 1

INTRODUCTION

"Who (what) is a professional counselor?" is a question that has been asked often by both professionals and laypersons. It is also a question that, although responded to by a wide variety of professionals, has never been adequately answered. The many attempts to provide an effective response usually have focused on counselors' personal characteristics, training, professional perspectives, and/or the roles counselors are expected to fulfill. For example, Brown and Srebalus (1988) wrote that "the general orientation of counselors to health and wellness, as opposed to psychopathology and mental illness . . . enables counselors to deal with the burgeoning mental health concerns of our society" (p. 14). Relatedly, Gibson and Mitchell (1986) indicated that

> we begin by identifying counseling as a helping profession; a concept that forms the basis for the role and function of the counselor in today's society. A "helping" profession may be described as one in which the members are especially trained and licensed or certificated to perform a unique and needed service for the fellow human beings of their society. (p. 23)

Gladding (1988) noted that "professional counselors obtain either a masters degree or a doctorate in counselor education" (p. 38). Peterson and Nisenholz (1987) indicated that a tendency toward selfactualization is a primary counselor characteristic and that "some additional characteristics that are particularly important in becoming a counselor include personal energy level, risk-taking ability, tolerance of ambiguity, authenticity, trustworthiness, and capacity for intimacy" (p. 9).

Many other authors (e.g., Belkin, 1988; Capuzzi & Gross, 1991; Lewis, Hayes, & Lewis, 1992; Nugent, 1990; Vacc & Loesch, 1993) also have addressed at some length the personal and professional characteristics, preparations, roles, functions, employment situations, orientations, and techniques of professional counselors. Collectively, they provide a "sense" of who or what a professional counselor is. However, this sense is incomplete as a response to the question because it does not encompass what it is that counselors actually *do* in their daily activities. There has not been a systematic, broad-scale, and analytically thorough investigation of the work behaviors (i.e., routinely used professional activities) of persons who identify themselves as professional counselors.

The Impetus for the Study

Intriguing as the resultant information may be, intrigue is not in and of itself sufficient justification for the great expenditures of time and money necessary to conduct an effective work behavior study (i.e., job analysis) for those who identify themselves as professional counselors. What *is* sufficient justification is professional and/or legal "mandates" to obtain the information.

The National Counselor Examination (NCE) has been used by the NBCC as an integral part of its general practice counselor certification process for about a decade. Since 1985, candidates for NBCC's "National Certified Counselor" (NCC) status have had to surpass a minimum criterion score on the NCE in order to become an NCC. Substantial empirical data have been accumulated to support the psychometric quality of the NCE for the purposes for which it is intended and used (Loesch & Vacc, 1991). Certainly, its psychometric properties and supporting evidence exceed those of other examinations used in some professional certification processes. The NCE is most acceptable, both professionally and legally, as a criterion within the context of the NBCC counselor certification process. However, the NCE is limited to the extent that, while it is grounded in accepted and widely recognized professional standards, it is not grounded in the results of job analysis. This situation precludes the NCE being a *direct* measure of counselors' work behaviors.

Although it is not legally essential, it is increasingly desirable that certification (or licensure) examinations be based on job analyses. Moreover, the most effective, and therefore most "defensible," professional credentialing examinations are derived from job analyses. In speculating about trends in testing in professional credentialing, Linn (1985) wrote that

> boards can expect that they will more likely be called upon to justify their procedures than was true in the past. Evidence of the validity of examinations for determining whether a candidate has the necessary knowledge, skills, and abilities for competent practice will be crucial in justifying the licensing [or certification] process. (p. 196)

Shimberg and Rosenfeld (1990) echoed this prediction:

> Traditionally, licensing board members or committees of subject matter experts (SMEs) have determined the knowledge and skills to be assessed. However, in recent years, there has been an increased emphasis on *verifying* the judgments of those SMEs by conducting job analysis studies. (p. 14)

Their comments have already come true to some extent. For example, in describing credentialing trends in California, an article in the newsletter of the Council on Licensure, Enforcement, and Regulation ("California Revamps Examinations Process, 1990") reported that

> in the last few years, many of the [California Consumer Affairs] department's [credentialing] boards and bureaus have created job-related licensing examinations, and reducing [*sic*] the time and costs involved, even when it is necessary to administer examinations more frequently. By conducting occupational analyses and deleting portions of exams that test for purely academic, outdated, or other non job-related information, the department feels it is making licensing examinations fair to applicants. It also feels that the public protection is increased when candidates are tested for job-related knowledge and skills. (p. 3)

Thus, there is a professional and perhaps legal impetus for conducting a job analysis to support the NCE or any future modification of it.

The desirability of credentialing examinations being grounded in a job analysis also is reflected in the AERA/APA/NCME *Standards for Educational and Psychological Testing* (APA, 1985). Standard 11.1 states, in part, that "a rationale should be provided to support a claim that the knowledge or skills being assessed are required for competent performance in an occupation" (APA, 1985, p. 64). The Comment section for this standard includes the following statements:

> Job analyses provide the primary basis for defining the content domain. . . . Although the job analysis techniques are comparable to those for employment testing, the emphasis for licensure or certification is limited appropriately to knowledge and skills necessary to protect the public. Generally, knowledge and skills contained in a core curriculum designed to train people for the job or occupation are relevant. (APA, 1985, p. 64)

Again, these statements both support the use of the NCE as it currently exists and emphasize the desirability of a job analysis for further development and evolution of the NCE.

What Is a Job Analysis?

Types of job analyses are differentiated by the focus of the investigative/analytic effort. Fine (1986) wrote:

> One difference in job analysis methodology . . . has been whether the method focused on what got done (i.e., was work oriented) or whether it focused on what the worker did (i.e., was

> worker oriented). Worker-oriented methods . . . are based on the notion that there is a finite set of dimensions, a taxonomy of aptitudes, abilities, or characteristics that can be used to describe a job and that accounts for the variability of human performance. (p. 53)

Counseling, as a professional activity, often has been described in terms of counselors' characteristics, skills, and abilities. Such a description has done much to clarify the nature of the profession. However, in view of the ever-increasing variety of activities and services conducted under the general rubric of "counseling," worker-oriented perspectives are becoming less and less exact, and therefore decreasing in value. Conversely, because of the diversification of counseling activities and services, a work-oriented description (that includes elements of commonality across those who are counselors) is desirable and therefore was the focus of this study.

In general, a "work-oriented" job analysis (sometimes referred to as a position analysis, an occupational analysis, or, herein, a work behavior study) is a systematic examination of the nature and/or elements of a relatively broadly defined (employment) "position," "occupation," or "job." In effect, a job analysis is an investigation of the degrees of dissimilarity or similarity in the work/vocational activities among individuals. When there is expectation of dissimilarity, a job analysis helps to clarify or delineate differences among the vocational activities of the individuals assessed. The resultant information may be used to clarify positional, job, or occupational definitions, the organizational/functional relationships among workers, and/or specifications of respective selection or evaluation criteria. When there is expectation of similarity, a job analysis helps to clarify degrees of congruence as well as relative emphases among work activities (Fine, 1986). The resultant information may be used to develop job definitions and/or selection and evaluation criteria.

Addressing the general purpose of a job analysis, Shimberg and Rosenfeld (1990) indicated that

> job analysis is a process that seeks information from a large number of incumbent practitioners regarding the:
>
> - most important aspects of the job; and
> - the knowledge and skills needed to perform the job in a safe and effective manner. (p. 14)

Regarding the potential benefits of a job analysis, Fine (1986) wrote that "job analysis can also provide the behaviors that might be used to construct selection tests, the knowledge and abilities that need to be incorporated in training curricula, and the relevant dimensions for assessment and diagnosis of performance" (p. 55). Although these comments provide perceptual parameters, they do not stipulate the manner in which a job analysis is to be conducted. Raymond (1990) noted that

> as just about every experienced job analyst knows, the practice of job analysis is more art than science. Perhaps that explains, in part, why job analyses are both interesting and challenging.
>
> There are many ways to conduct a job analysis, and many of the decisions about a job analysis are based on educated guesses, usually good ones, on how best to proceed. (p. 9)

Thus, job analyses are conducted to fulfill specific, individualized purposes; there is not a singular, prescribed method of conducting a job analysis.

Three major categories of decisions must be considered in conducting a job analysis: (a) conceptual, (b) procedural, and (c) analytical. Each are discussed below.

Conceptual decisions. Conceptual decisions are related to issues such as the purposes of the job analysis, situational contexts for the investigation, type of information desired, and potential uses of the results (including characteristics and qualifications of users/consumers). For example, in addressing the use of job analyses as the bases for credentialing examinations, Smith and Hambleton (1990) indicated that

> licensure [and certification] examinations are *not* designed to predict future job success, which is difficult to assess at any time and nearly impossible to do well when candidates are working in many different settings and jobs. Rather, licensure [and certification] examinations are intended to identify candidates who are deficient in certain essential knowledge and skill areas at the time of entry into their professions. (p. 7)

They also noted that

> a present concern among some legislators and measurement specialists is how to ensure that sponsors of licensure [or certification] examination programs conduct appropriate validation research, and use results in reasonable ways to make needed changes in examination content and item format. (Smith & Hambleton, 1990, p. 8)

In general, a job analysis as a basis for a credentialing examination is intended to allow for development of a "test blueprint" from which the examination can be developed; that is, to identify the domains of performance for a particular occupation so that items can be developed that reflect those domains (Raymond, 1990).

Procedural decisions. Procedural decisions are related to issues such as general research methodology (including appropriate sample size, sampling procedures, and item generation) and task (i.e., item response) format. Item generation issues are centered on the specificity of the job tasks (i.e., work behaviors) included in the survey as well as the nature of the information about those tasks given to the respondents (Harvey & Lozada-Larsen, 1988). Task (response) format issues have been the focus of much discussion in the professional literature. According to Raymond (1990), "most job analysis surveys consist of rating scales such as *frequency*, *criticality*, *complexity*, *difficulty of learning*, and *time spent*" (p. 10). Frequency and criticality (i.e., importance) ratings for various job tasks are the most commonly obtained information (Kane, Kingsbury, Colton, & Estes, 1989).

Analytical decisions. The issues related to data-analytic procedures have been focused on the actual statistical procedures used (see Harvey, 1986) and methods used to "combine" various types of ratings obtained (cf. Kane et al., 1989; Sanchez & Levine, 1989). With regard to the former, exploratory, descriptive (as opposed to inferential) statistical procedures are preferred in the absence of clearly defined groupings of occupational entities (Harvey, 1986). In regard to the latter, the technique of choice depends on the assumptions to be used by the consumers of the resultant information.

In sum, it is obvious that there are no "hard-and-fast" rules about how a job analysis, is to be conducted. Rather, for any job analysis, there are a variety of issues to be considered and a corresponding number of decisions to be made dependent upon the unique purposes and circumstances for the study. The study described here was conducted to strengthen the NCE. Additional factors influencing the methodology of this study were potentials for use of the NCE in contexts other than the NBCC's certification process (e.g., within state counselor licensure procedures) and for other professional purposes (e.g., for consideration in regard to professional preparation standards or for research).

Basic Premises for the Study

Several basic premises were established prior to initiation of this study. First, it was decided that the "final" respondent pool would be limited to NCCs. This premise was theoretically and professionally appropriate because the NCC population represents a broad spectrum of persons who identify themselves as professional counselors. Various NCCs work in almost all professional settings in which counselors are employed, including public and private community agency, edu-cational, business, and other settings. Counselors working in private practice also are represented. Furthermore, included among NCCs are counselors having a wide variety of academic and other professional credentials. Therefore, rather than limit representation, the "restriction" to NCCs in fact broadens the representation of the study.

It should be noted that although the final respondent sample was limited to NCCs, input from other professionals also was valued. In particular, because of the similarity in the philosophical and professional orientations of the NBCC and the American Counseling Association (ACA), opportunities for input were provided to ACA members in the early stages of the study.

A second premise for the study was that it would be focused on actual work behaviors engaged in by professional counselors (i.e., work oriented rather than worker oriented), and, to the greatest extent possible, those work behaviors would be contributed by counseling practitioners. Relatedly, it was understood that every effort would be made to investigate work behaviors stipulated as specifically as possible.

That the approach used was to be "exploratory" in nature was the third premise underlying the study. That is, no predetermined sets or groups of counselors' work behaviors were assumed. A considerable number of "role-and-function" statements for professional counselors exist. However, each is restricted to counselors having a stipulated title (e.g., school, rehabilitation, mental health, or marriage/family counselors) or a stipulated setting (e.g., elementary, middle, or secondary schools; colleges or universities; business and industry; or community agencies). Thus, the approach was to focus on what they were doing as opposed to general statements of what they were supposed to be doing.

A fourth premise was that the study would be focused on work behaviors presumed to be common among all professional counselors. Numerous "specialties" exist among those who identify themselves as professional counselors, with variations usually reflected in titles or work settings. Examination of work behaviors unique to a particular setting was far beyond the scope of this study. Therefore, the premise here was to investigate generic work behaviors engaged in, at least to some extent, by the vast majority of professional counselors.

Chapter 2

METHODOLOGY

In order to conduct the study in accord with the underlying premises, it was necessary that the study proceed in a series of "phases." These phases were most evident in the development of the survey used and its eventual distribution to the respondent sample of NCCs.

Phase 1: Initial Item Generation

The purpose of the first phase of the study was to develop a list of work behaviors *potentially* suitable for inclusion in the survey. This purpose was fulfilled through two methods: a review of related professional literature and materials and a general solicitation of counselors' professional work behaviors.

Professional materials. The process of identifying potentially suitable work behavior statements through existing professional materials followed three parallel paths. The first involved a systematic search of published professional literature using computerized search methods. This search yielded a wide variety of professional documents purported to be focused on counselors' activities. Unfortunately, the vast majority of these documents were rather general "role and function" statements for various types of counselors. That is, most of the "function" elements identified within them were global characterizations of sets of more specific activities. Therefore, only a few specific, potentially suitable work behavior statements were gleaned from these sources; for the most part, the "function" statements in them were too general to fit the purposes of the study.

A computerized search for job analysis studies of persons in the "helping" professions similarly was not particularly fruitful. Unfortunately, only a very few job analyses for "helping" professionals are contained in the published professional literature. Even more unfortunately, those presented have been focused either on very narrowly defined aspects of the counseling profession or on very limited and restricted samples, thus having relatively limited generalizability. Even Fitzgerald and Osipow's (1986) job analysis for counseling psychologists did not contain items deemed specific enough for the study. However, these sources did serve to generate ideas for some potentially useful statements.

The second approach to using existing professional materials involved a review of various "competency statements" for counseling professionals. Again, many of the sets of competencies reviewed were specific to particular counseling specialties and, therefore, did not contain many potentially generalizable work behavior statements. However, one set that did contain some possibly useful statements was that published by the American Personnel and Guidance Association (now ACA) (Dameron, 1980). It was also very useful as a model for structuring work behavior statements.

The third approach to using existing professional materials was a review of job analysis materials that had been used for related but relatively specific purposes. This included (a) a survey used in a job analysis for psychologists that was conducted by ETS on behalf of the American Association of State Psychology Boards, (b) a job analysis survey used by the Minnesota Personnel and Guidance Association in 1981, (c) a mental health counselors' task analysis survey used by the Florida Department of Professional Regulation (1987) in the development of that state's mental health counselor licensure examination, and (d) a survey used for a job analysis for alcoholism and drug abuse counselors (National Association of Alcoholism and Drug Abuse Counselors, 1986). Most of the items used on these and other surveys were deemed either irrelevant to the generic work of counselors, too general, too specific, or dated (i.e., they no longer reflected current professional practices). However, these and similar documents served to provide ideas for some items, suggestions for item structuring, and potentially appropriate survey formats.

Solicitation of work behaviors. The second major potential-item generation method was solicitation of work behavior statements from practicing counselors. A counselors' work behavior statement solicitation announcement (Appendix A) appropriate for a variety of professional publications and other methods of distribution was developed for this purpose.

Because the study was to focus on NCCs, the announcement was first published in the Spring 1989 issue of the NBCC newsletter, *Newsnotes*, which was distributed to approximately 17,000 NCCs. However, because it was desirable to obtain input (i.e., work behavior statements) from a wide variety of professional counselors, the announcement also was distributed in other ways. One primary distribution was its publication in two issues of the *Guidepost* sent to approximately 55,000 ACA (formerly AACD) members in the spring of 1989. It also was distributed in the spring of 1989 to the newsletter editors of all ACA membership divisions and all ACA branches (e.g., state divisions), along with a request that it be printed as soon as possible. It was impractical to monitor all these publications, but it was determined that at least 10 of the then 13 ACA division newsletters printed the announcement. Requests for use of other methods of distribution of the announcement to counseling professionals also were sent to each of the presidents of the 13 ACA divisions. Again, it was not possible to monitor exactly the impact of this approach, but it was determined that some of the ACA division presidents made specific efforts to distribute the announcements to divisional credentialing/standards or other appropriate committees for their input.

The announcement also was printed in the fall 1989 issue of *Connections*, the newsletter of the Council for the Accreditation of Counseling and Related Educational Programs (CACREP). This was distributed to the faculty of approximately 55 counselor preparation programs having one or more CACREP accredited programs, as well as other professionals who have been integrally involved in CACREP's activities. Finally, the announcement was sent, along with a request for distribution, to approximately 45 members of the American Association of State Counselor [licensure] Boards (AASCB). Again, although the total dissemination from this tactic is unknown, at least 10 state counselor licensure boards distributed the announcement to licensed professional counselors (or similarly titled individuals) in their states.

By the late fall of 1989, slightly over 400 pieces of correspondence had been received in response to the distributions of the work behavior statements solicitation announcements. The diversity among the materials submitted was unexpected. For example, submitted were professional position descriptions, "objectives" from syllabi of completed counselor education courses, formal descriptions of the programs in which the counselor worked, references for "role and function" statements, agency or school system accountability criteria statements and descriptions, and locally developed competency statements. Fortunately, the vast majority of the respondents submitted work behavior statements that were in accord with the guidelines in the announcement and, therefore, poten-tially useful for the study. Although most respondents provided less than 10 work behavior statements, the cumulative result was a list of approximately 500 statements for consideration.

The next step in this phase was "pooling" the statements from the solicitation announcements with those derived from the review of the professional literature and materials. As expected, a vast majority of the statements from the professional literature and materials were represented among the statements submitted in response to the solicitation announcement.

The last step in this phase was a critical review by the researchers to cull from the list those statements that were clearly inappropriate. Statements that essentially duplicated other statements on the list were eliminated. More important, items that were not stated as *behaviors* were eliminated. It should be noted that while this activity was conducted to "clean up" the list, every effort was made to retain items so that the list would be as comprehensive as possible. For example, some statements were easily modified to be behavioral in nature. The result of this effort was a list of 329 counselor work behavior statements deemed potentially appropriate for inclusion in the survey.

Phase 2: Item Refinement

The purpose of the second phase of the study was to identify the counselor work behavior statements to be included on the survey by reducing the number on the original list. It was decided that feedback and input from practicing professional counselors was essential to this process.

There were two parts to this phase of the study. In the first part, a cover letter (Appendix B) and the initial list of work behavior statements (Appendix C) were sent to all ACA membership division officers listed in the 1990 ACA directory and to the practitioner member representatives of the AASCB; the materials were not sent to AASCB members who were employees of a state counselor licensure regulatory agency. The assistance of the ACA membership division officers was desired because they represented active and professionally involved practitioners holding professional orientations known to be in accord with those of ACA and, relatedly, NBCC. The assistance of the AASCB practitioner members was desired because they represented a variety of counseling practitioners, ones who were obviously deeply involved in the credentialing of counselors.

A total of 71 counseling professionals received the request letter and list. In general, they were requested to modify and/or edit the list in any way they deemed appropriate; they were not given specific instructions for modifying the list (see Appendix B). Usable responses were received from 28 professionals (a 39% return rate). Their feedback suggestions took a variety of forms, including suggestions for elimination of items, combining of items, and rewriting of items. A few additional items also were suggested.

The feedback from these professionals was reviewed by the researchers with the intent of summarizing suggestions and recommendations. One component of this process was determining the frequency of retention or deletion recommendations for each item. The results of these determinations are presented in Appendix C. It should be noted that there was a degree of subjectivity in the counting of the retention or deletion recommendations. For example, some suggestions to combine items were extremely complex, and some relatively subjective decisions had to be made about how best to count the individual item recommendations. Also, suggested modifications (e.g., editing or other refinements) that were incorporated influenced the ways retention or deletion recommendations were counted. However, despite the minor degree of subjectivity in determining the respective item counts, the resultant item frequency counts served as the primary basis for developing the list of work behavior statements actually included in the survey.

Phase 3: Survey Construction and Distribution

The result of the first two phases of the study was a list of 151 counselor work behavior statements deemed suitable for inclusion in the survey. The survey materials consisted of a cover letter, instructions for completion and return of the survey, the eight-page survey (i.e., four two-sided pages suitable for optical scanning), and a return-addressed, postage-paid envelope (see Appendix D).

The demographic data requested from the respondents included type of highest degree held in counseling preparation (see Step 1, part a), primary work setting (see Step 1, part b), and gender, licensures, and other certifications (items 153, 154, and 155 on the Importance form, respectively).

In listing the items on the survey form, item 100 was inadvertently omitted. Thus, 151, rather than 152, items were actually included in the survey. The respondents were requested to respond to the set of 151 work behavior statements twice. They first indicated, on a 5-point response scale (1 = never, 2 = rarely, 3 = occasionally, 4 = frequently, and 5 = routinely), the relative FREQUENCY in which they engaged in each of the various work behaviors. Second, they indicated, again on a 5-point response scale (1 = of no importance, 2 = of little importance, 3 = moderately important, 4 = very important, and 5 = critically important), the relative IMPORTANCE (i.e., level of crucialness) that their counselees would place on their being able to perform the respective work behaviors effectively.

Numerous authors (e.g., Borg & Gall, 1989; Eichelberger, 1989;

Glasnapp & Poggio, 1985; Hays, 1988; Howell, 1989; Kachigan, 1986; Kraemer & Theimann, 1987; Lipsey, 1990; Schafer, 1990; Thompson, 1989) have discussed the relationships among statistical power, effect size, and sample size and have made recommendations for how to determine the minimum sample size needed for various research endeavors. In general, (a) information from previous research should be used whenever possible, (b) desired criteria and practical considerations should mitigate final decisions, and (c) the larger the sample size, the better (Borg & Gall, 1989; Kraemer & Theimann, 1987).

Unfortunately, as previously noted, large-scale, generally representative job analyses among persons who identify themselves as professional counselors have not been conducted. Thus, there was not a directly relevant research basis for calculating the desired sample size for the study. However, based on the *assumption* that response variation among counseling psychologists would not be radically different from that among counselors, the Fitzgerald and Osipow (1986) study provided some information upon which to base an estimate.

Fitzgerald and Osipow (1986) conducted a job analysis for counseling psychologists (in part) in regard to importance and relative time spent in (i.e., frequency of behavior) each of 64 work behaviors. Responses were made on 7-point, Likert-type scales. The mean standard deviations were 1.84 for the importance responses and 1.73 for the time spent responses. The average of these standard deviations is 1.79. A proportionate conversion of this standard deviation for a 5-point scale is achieved by solving the equation $(1.79/7) = (x/5)$. The result is a proportionately equivalent standard deviation of 1.28.

Because factor analysis was to be the primary data-analytic technique for the study, the sample size needed for effective factor analysis was an important consideration. Many authors have provided suggestions for minimum sample sizes for effective factor analysis, but clearly there is no consensus among them. In general, it is recommended that the number of respondents be five (or more) times the number of items and/or a minimum of 100.

Kachigan (1986, p. 157) presented the formula $N = ([(z)\ (SD)]/E)^2$ to estimate a desired sample size. In this formula, z is the unit normal value associated with the desired confidence level, SD is the standard deviation estimate, and E is the specified acceptable error. Using the very conservative estimate of error of no more than .10 response units in estimating population means, at the .05 level (i.e., $z = 1.96$), the needed sample size is given by $N = ([(1.96)$

X (1.28)]/.10)^2 = 630. Although this is a relatively inexact and conservative (i.e., necessitating a larger sample size) method of estimating, it did suggest that a minimum of approximately 630 respondents was needed for the study.

No specifically pertinent data on return rates for survey research among professional counselors were found in the professional literature. However, return rates of approximately one third are not uncommon. Therefore, the survey was distributed to approximately 1,500 NCCs in March 1991, based on the assumption that this distribution would yield a sufficient sample size. The 1,500 survey recipients constituted an approximately 10% randomly selected sample of the then approximately 15,500 NCCs who were fully active (i.e., had fulfilled all candidacy and/or continuing education requirements for current NCC status). All usable (i.e., correctly completed) surveys returned by June 1, 1991, were included for subsequent analysis.

Chapter 3

RESPONDENT AND RESPONSE DATA

A total of 722 NCCs returned surveys from which usable data could be obtained, representing a return rate of approximately 48% (i.e., 722/1,500). Ten other surveys were returned with notations indicating that while the recipients were currently NCCs, they were not active as counselors and therefore did not believe it appropriate to complete the survey. Unfortunately, some of the respondents failed to respond to all items as requested, resulting in a total of 694 returned surveys with responses to all of the work behavior statement items. This number exceeded the conservatively estimated minimum sample size needed for valid generalization and statistical power considerations and was suitable for factor analysis considerations for the study. All statistical analyses for the study were conducted using the Statistical Package for the Social Sciences Version X (SPSSX) computer programs.

Shown in Table 1 are the self-reported demographic data for the respondents.

Table 1
Respondents' Demographic Data

Category	*n*
Gender	
Males	206
Females	476
Not specified	40
Total	722
Highest academic degree held	
Master's degree - counseling	405
Master's degree - closely related area	53
Education specialist - counseling	52
Education specialist - closely related area	12
Doctoral degree - counselor education	66
Doctoral degree - counseling psychology	41
Doctoral degree - other closely related area	52
Not specified	41
Primary professional work setting(s)	
Academic (CACREP-approved program)	25
Academic (non-CACREP approved program)	20
School	160
Postsecondary institution	64
Counseling center	43
Hospital	22
Research facility	1
Government agency	34
Private industry	19
Community mental health center	57
Private practice	135
Full-time counselor	23
Not specified	119
Licensures	
Professional counselor (or equivalent title)	331
Psychologist	14
Marriage/family counselor	15
Other certifications	
NCCC	7
AAMFT	7
CCMHC	18
CRC	78
School	29

Approximately 30% of the respondents were male and 70% were female. Approximately 63% of the respondents had a master's degree, 9% had completed an education specialist degree, and 22% had a doctorate; 6% did not indicate their highest degree held. Approximately 43% of the respondents reported working in "educational" settings, 41% reported working in noneducation settings, and 16% provided no response concerning their primary work setting. Fifty percent of the respondents indicated having a professional license, with 46% of all respondents being licensed as a professional counselor (or equivalent title). Only 19% of the respondents indicated holding a certification in addition to being an NCC, with the most common certification (11% of all respondents) being a Certified Rehabilitation Counselor (CRC).

Because all respondents were NCCs, they were considered professional counselors. Therefore, primary interest was in the aggregate data generated, not in subgroup differences based on various demographic characteristics. However, secondary data analyses were conducted to investigate such differences in order to gain supplementary information about response patterns. Since a disproportionate distribution of respondents existed across some of the demographic characteristic categories, and to simplify these secondary analyses, the types of demographic information obtained were collapsed into dichotomies. The results indicated the following about the respondents: (a) 522 had entry-level and 159 had doctoral degrees and (b) 355 were in educational and 268 in job settings.

The numbers of respondents selecting the different FREQUENCY and IMPORTANCE ratings are presented in Appendices E and F, respectively. Those responding to each work behavior concerning its frequency of performance and level of importance and the mean rating and standard deviation are presented in Tables 2 and 3, respectively.

Among the FREQUENCY data, the five items having the highest means were (a) use "active listening" skills (item 34, mean = 4.77); (b) maintain case notes, records, and/or files (item 10, mean = 4.51); (c) establish counseling goals (item 13, mean = 4.44); (d) clarify client's support systems (item 6, mean = 4.34); and (e) evaluate client's movement toward counseling goals (item 44, mean = 4.33).

The five work behaviors performed least frequently were (a) engage in field/observational research (item 120, mean = 1.80), (b) provide career counseling for children (item 102, mean = 1.74), (c) evaluate computer software (item 127, mean = 1.64), (d) conduct fund-raising

Table 2
Number Responding to Each Work Behavior Statement With Mean Rating and Standard Deviation for FREQUENCY of Performance

Item	Number Responding	Mean Rating[a]	(*SD*)
1. Obtain client's informed consent prior to counseling	715	3.80	1.50
2. Evaluate existing pre-counseling) client data	720	4.07	1.10
3. Develop compre-hensivetreatment plans	717	3.55	1.30
4. Assess psychosocial	717	4.02	1.08
5. Assess potential for client to harm self/others	722	4.13	1.17
6. Clarify client's support systems	722	4.34	0.87
7. Systematically ob-serve client behaviors	721	4.23	1.01
8. Assist with client's evaluation of counseling	715	3.59	1.19
9. Self-evaluate coun-seling effectiveness	713	4.30	0.87
10. Maintain case notes, records, and/or files	716	4.51	0.96
11. Conduct former client follow-up activities	720	2.86	1.11
12. Conduct precoun-seling diagnostic interview	719	3.23	1.37
13. Establish counseling goals	720	4.44	0.89
14. Analyze cost-benefit of treatment alternatives	715	2.56	1.34
15. Determine DSM-III-R classification	712	2.71	1.59
16. Evaluate extent of client's psychological dysfunction	711	3.59	1.41
17. Reframe client's problem	715	3.99	1.04
18. Use computerized "coun-seling" software	713	1.85	1.20
19. Counsel short-term (less than 6 sessions)	719	3.60	1.10
20. Counsel long-term (6 sessions or longer)	717	3.62	1.17
21. Interview client's significant others	721	3.00	1.08
22. Research use of a specific counseling intervention	713	2.79	1.06
23. Counsel children	719	2.73	1.54
24. Counsel adolescents	719	3.55	1.31
25. Counsel adults	721	4.17	1.03
26. Counselor older persons	719	2.72	1.25
27. Counsel persons in crisis	716	3.72	0.98
28. Counsel clients concerning substance use/abuse	714	3.16	1.17
29. Counsel clients concerning personal change	718	4.20	0.91
30. Counsel clients concerning physical abuse	716	3.10	1.09
31. Counsel clients concerning life-style change	721	3.65	1.06
32. Counsel clients concerning personality change	719	3.18	1.13
33. Counsel clients concerning sexual abuse	721	3.04	1.16
34. Use "active listening" skills	716	4.77	0.54

Item	Number Responding	Mean Rating[a]	(*SD*)
35. Use affective-oriented counseling techniques	714	4.02	0.95
36. Use behavioral-oriented counseling techniques	720	3.86	0.92
37. Use cognitive-oriented counseling techniques	719	3.94	0.93
38. Use brief psychotherapy techniques	708	3.11	1.20
39. Use media resources in counseling	718	2.92	1.09
40. Inform client about human growth and development	720	3.79	0.94
41. Inform client about ethical standards and practice	717	3.75	1.17
42. Inform client about legal aspects of counseling	715	3.21	1.23
43. Evaluate need for client referral	716	4.16	0.94
44. Evaluate client's movement toward counseling goals	714	4.33	0.89
45. Clarify counselor/client roles	713	3.95	1.02
46. Clarify client's moral/spiritual issues	710	3.14	1.15
47. Identify source-of-problem alternatives	706	3.91	0.93
48. Identify client's non-counseling resources	715	3.96	0.93
49. Provide human development education	710	3.45	1.02
50. Provide career vocational education	715	3.35	1.22
51. Provide mental health enhancement training/education	718	3.14	1.88

Item	Number Responding	Mean Rating[a]	(*SD*)
52. Prepare developmental/preventative media	714	2.41	1.19
53. Conduct prevention-oriented developmental activities	715	2.95	1.21
54. Conduct self-development training for nonclients	713	2.61	1.23
55. Provide multicultural training/education	718	2.28	1.22
56. Participate in case conferences	715	3.57	1.25
57. Provide consultation services for organizational development	716	2.53	1.24
58. Provide consultation services for human relationships development	715	2.71	1.21
59. Provide consultation services for interpersonal skills training	711	2.79	1.20
60. Provide consultation services for human resource needs evaluation	715	2.31	1.15
61. Provide consultation services for ethical or legal dilemmas	717	2.02	1.10
62. Provide consultation services for professional skill development	714	2.70	1.22
63. Inform family members of family counseling guidelines and goals	717	3.07	1.30
64. Inform family of family dynamics/roles	716	3.08	1.28
65. Clarify familial behavior norms	714	3.04	1.28
66. Clarify family counseling goals	715	2.97	1.37

Item	Number Responding	Mean Rating[a]	(*SD*)
67. Develop family conflict resolution strategies	705	3.04	1.33
68. Use the following family counseling techniques: multigenerational	706	2.39	1.26
69. Use the following family counseling techniques: structural	706	2.49	1.25
70. Use the following family counseling techniques: strategic	707	2.42	1.23
71. Use the following family counseling techniques: behavioral	709	2.70	1.30
72. Counsel concerning premarriage	711	2.07	1.07
73. Counsel concerning divorce	710	2.77	1.23
74. Counsel concerning divorce-conflict reduction	705	2.60	1.21
75. Counsel concerning human sexuality	707	2.74	1.17
76. Counsel concerning marriage enrichment	705	2.39	1.26
77. Counsel concerning family change	710	3.18	1.15
78. Counsel concerning family member interaction	707	3.38	1.17
79. Inform clients of group counseling guidelines and goals	710	3.40	1.42
80. Systematically observe group members' behaviors	712	3.49	1.45
81. Identify harmful group-member behaviors	719	3.40	1.42

Item	Number Responding	Mean Rating[a]	(*SD*)
82. Evaluate progress toward group goals	715	3.45	1.41
83. Resolve conflict among group members	717	3.24	1.34
84. Assist with group members' feedback to each other	719	3.44	1.39
85. Determine group counseling termination criteria	721	3.26	1.45
86. Self-evaluate group counseling effectiveness	718	3.47	1.45
87. Use "structured" activities during group counseling	715	3.18	1.32
88. Use leader-centered group counseling leadership techniques	716	2.93	1.23
89. Use group-centered group counseling leadership techniques	717	3.07	1.27
90. Use laissez-faire group counseling leadership techniques	713	2.08	1.01
91. Evaluate client's occupational skills	722	3.00	1.32
92. Evaluate client's educational preparations	721	3.56	1.24
93. Facilitate client's development of decision-making skills	720	4.02	0.92
94. Facilitate client's development of job-search skills	722	2.98	1.28
95. Provide group vocational counseling	720	2.23	1.35
96. Provide outplacement counseling	713	1.97	1.25
97. Use occupational information	719	2.95	1.46
98. Use computerized career counseling resources	716	2.29	1.49

Item	Number Responding	Mean Rating[a]	(*SD*)
99. Use career resources library	719	2.54	1.48
100. (Omitted on questionnaire)			
101. Use print and other media in career counseling	715	2.72	1.50
102. Provide career counseling for children	716	1.74	1.15
103. Provide career counseling for adolescents	720	2.61	1.45
104. Provide career counseling for adults	719	2.69	1.42
105. Provide career counseling for older adults	716	2.05	1.29
106. Provide career counseling for persons with disabilities	719	2.26	1.33
107. Select appraisal instruments/techniques for counseling	711	2.94	1.35
108. Use test results for client decision making	719	3.13	1.33
109. Assist client in understanding test results	718	3.49	1.37
110. Use test/inventory results for intervention selections	714	2.98	1.29
111. Use aptitude tests	717	2.55	1.43
112. Use achievement tests	722	2.64	1.49
113. Use interest inventories	722	2.94	1.43
114. Use self-report personality inventories	722	2.91	1.31
115. Use intelligence tests	713	2.39	1.35
116. Use nontest appraisal techniques	716	2.76	1.42
117. Engage in needs assessment	718	3.09	1.28
118. Engage in counseling process research	721	1.96	1.12
119. Engage in counseling outcome research	721	1.95	1.11
120. Engage in field/observational research	720	1.80	1.05
121. Engage in experimental/laboratory research	718	1.35	0.72
122. Engage in formative evaluation of counseling program	709	2.61	1.34
123. Engage in summative evaluation of counseling program	703	2.63	1.35
124. Engage in data analyses	709	2.29	1.27
125. Collaborate in research with other professionals	710	2.15	1.19
126. Develop appraisal instrument/technique	710	1.87	1.08
127. Evaluate computer software	705	1.64	1.00
128. Provide expert witness testimony	709	1.84	1.03
129. Participate in professional organization activities	708	3.66	1.15
130. Participate in continuing education/skill enhancement	707	4.30	0.88
131. Write for publication	706	1.95	1.13
132. Write communication for non-counseling, professional activities	706	2.35	1.27

Item	Number Responding	Mean Rating[a]	(*SD*)
133. Review ethical standards	712	2.76	1.16
134. Supervise counselor trainees	713	2.57	1.37
135. Read current professional literature	708	4.11	0.92
136. Review legal statutes and regulations	711	3.09	1.14
137. Assess programmatic needs	707	3.30	1.23
138. Establish programmatic service goals	702	3.16	1.31
139. Participate in staffing decision-making processes	706	3.56	1.38
140. Allocate financial resources for counseling program	707	2.28	1.49
141. Administer counseling program	709	2.84	1.69
142. Use computers for program data management	707	2.20	1.47
143. Conduct fund-raising activities for program development/maintenance	712	1.49	0.92
144. Develop program-related reports	708	2.71	1.40
145. Correspond orally with others to maintain communication	710	4.31	0.97
146. Write to other professionals to maintain communication	710	3.35	1.25
147. Evaluate counselors' performance	706	2.71	1.47
148. Provide counselor skill-development training	705	2.75	1.36
149. Serve as liaison with other agencies	708	3.41	1.30
150. Engage in professional/community public relations	707	3.40	1.25
151. Conduct community outreach	708	2.90	1.33
152. Supervise staff	704	2.64	1.61

[a]Response choices: 1 = never, 2 = rarely, 3 = occasionally, 4 = frequently, 5 = routinely.

Table 3
Number Responding to Each Work Behavior Statement With Mean Rating and Standard Deviation for IMPORTANCE of Each Behavior

Item	Number Responding	Mean Rating[a]	(*SD*)
1. Obtain client's informed consent prior to counseling	710	3.35	1.38
2. Evaluate existing (pre-counseling) client data	710	3.47	1.09
3. Develop comprehensive treatment plans	711	3.46	1.15
4. Assess psychosocial needs	709	3.67	1.07
5. Assess potential for client to harm self/others	707	4.09	1.16
6. Clarify client's support systems	708	3.87	0.94
7. Systematically observe behaviors	708	3.71	1.07
8. Assist with client's evaluation of counseling	708	3.54	1.06

Item	Number Responding	Mean Rating[a]	(*SD*)
9. Self-evaluate counseling effectiveness	711	3.78	1.10
10. Maintain case notes, records, and/or files	707	3.58	1.22
11. Conduct former client follow-up activities	710	2.83	1.05
12. Conduct precounseling diagnostic interview	709	3.06	1.19
13. Establish counseling goals	710	4.06	0.90
14. Analyze cost-benefit of treatment alternatives	707	2.92	1.34
15. Determine DSM-III-R classification	700	2.29	1.26
16. Evaluate extent of client's psychological dysfunction	710	3.57	1.26
17. Reframe client's problem	709	3.70	0.96
18. Use computerized "counseling" software	699	1.90	1.04
19. Counsel short-term (less than 6 sessions)	708	3.47	1.09
20. Counsel long-term (6 sessions or longer)	705	3.41	1.07
21. Interview client's significant others	711	3.02	1.02
22. Research use of a specific counseling intervention	703	2.51	1.16
23. Counsel children	704	3.04	1.55
24. Counsel adolescents	706	3.77	1.29
25. Counsel adults	703	4.09	1.03
26. Counsel older persons	701	3.50	1.33

Item	Number Responding	Mean Rating[a]	(*SD*)
27. Counsel persons in crisis	705	4.40	0.93
28. Counsel clients concerning substance use/abuse	700	3.79	1.17
29. Counsel clients concerning personal change	707	4.19	0.88
30. Counsel clients concerning physical abuse	705	3.92	1.16
31. Counsel clients concerning life-style change	707	3.86	1.04
32. Counsel clients concerning personality change	706	3.65	1.12
33. Counsel clients concerning sexual abuse	706	3.91	1.20
34. Use "active listening" skills	708	4.54	0.77
35. Use affective-oriented counseling techniques	703	3.77	1.09
36. Use behavioral-oriented counseling techniques	706	3.64	1.05
37. Use cognitive-oriented counseling techniques	705	3.68	1.04
38. Use brief psychotherapy techniques	704	3.16	1.21
39. Use media resources in counseling	708	2.74	1.13
40. Inform client about human growth and development	710	3.50	1.00
41. Inform client about ethical standards and practice	706	3.32	1.17
42. Inform client about legal aspects of counseling	704	3.09	1.17
43. Evaluate need for client referral	703	3.82	1.00
44. Evaluate client's movement toward counseling goals	703	4.04	0.91

Item	Number Responding	Mean Rating[a]	(*SD*)
45. Clarify counselor/client roles	702	3.85	0.98
46. Clarify client's moral/spiritual issues	702	3.10	1.10
47. Identify source-of-problem alternatives	698	3.85	0.92
48. Identify client's non-counseling resources	694	3.64	0.97
49. Provide human development education	697	3.21	1.03
50. Provide career/vocational education	698	3.25	1.28
51. Provide mental health enhancement training/education	704	3.00	1.14
52. Prepare developmental/preventative media	703	2.41	1.14
53. Conduct prevention-oriented developmental activities	700	2.94	1.15
54. Conduct self-development training for nonclients	698	2.32	1.16
55. Provide multicultural training/education	703	2.45	1.21
56. Participate in case conferences	701	3.12	1.28
57. Provide consultation services for organizational development	697	2.33	1.24
58. Provide consultation services for human relationships development	697	2.63	1.25
59. Provide consultation services for interpersonal skills training	699	2.72	1.24
60. Provide consultation services for human resource needs evaluation	696	2.42	1.20
61. Provide consultation services for ethical or legal dilemmas	699	2.36	1.17
62. Provide consultation services for professional skill development	695	2.49	1.23
63. Inform family members of family counseling guidelines and goals	701	3.17	1.21
64. Inform family of family dynamics/roles	701	3.19	1.19
65. Clarify familial behavior norms	701	3.20	1.16
66. Clarify family counseling goals	697	3.29	1.29
67. Develop family conflict resolution strategies	696	3.53	1.25
68. Use the following family counseling techniques: multigenerational	697	2.54	1.24
69. Use the following family counseling techniques: structural	697	2.56	1.21
70. Use the following family counseling techniques: strategic	694	2.57	1.21
71. Use the following family counseling techniques: behavioral	697	2.78	1.29
72. Counsel concerning premarriage	702	2.54	1.24
73. Counsel concerning divorce	703	3.19	1.26
74. Counsel concerning divorce-conflict reduction	695	3.21	1.30

Item	Number Responding	Mean Rating[a]	(SD)
75. Counsel concerning human sexuality	695	3.17	1.23
76. Counsel concerning marriage enrichment	695	2.80	1.33
77. Counsel concerning family change	698	3.52	1.14
78. Counsel concerning family member interaction	695	3.65	1.12
79. Inform clients of group counseling guidelines and goals	697	3.36	1.30
80. Systematically observe group members' behaviors	697	3.22	1.33
81. Identify harmful group-member behaviors	703	3.67	1.32
82. Evaluate progress toward group goals	701	3.51	1.26
83. Resolve conflict among group members	703	3.66	1.25
84. Assist with group members' feedback to each other	700	3.63	1.25
85. Determine group counseling termination criteria	699	3.32	1.28
86.Self-evaluate group counseling effectiveness	698	3.29	1.26
87. Use "structured" activities during group counseling	699	3.11	1.15
88. Use leader-centered group counseling leadership techniques	696	3.04	1.14
89. Use group-centered group counseling leadership techniques	695	3.12	1.15

Item	Number Responding	Mean Rating[a]	(SD)
90. Use laissez-faire group counseling leadership techniques	694	2.27	1.06
91. Evaluate client's occupational skills	706	3.01	1.32
92. Evaluate client's educational preparations	701	3.37	1.27
93. Facilitate client's development of decision-making skills	704	3.91	0.97
94. Facilitate client's development of job-search skills	701	3.06	1.29
95. Provide group vocational counseling	703	2.55	1.35
96. Provide outplacement counseling	700	2.36	1.32
97. Use occupational information	702	2.94	1.42
98. Use computerized career counseling resources	704	2.42	1.37
99. Use career resources library	704	2.59	1.41
100. (Omitted on questionnaire)			
101. Use print and other media in career counseling	702	2.68	1.37
102. Provide career counseling for children	701	2.01	1.20
103. Provide career counseling for adolescents	702	2.93	1.43
104. Provide career counseling for adults	699	2.98	1.47
105. Provide career counseling for older adults	703	2.50	1.37
106. Provide career counseling for persons with disabilities	699	2.81	1.44

Item	Number Responding	Mean Rating[a]	(*SD*)
107. Select appraisal instruments/techniques for counseling	701	2.94	1.32
108. Use test results for client decision making	707	3.18	1.25
109. Assist client in understanding test results	702	3.62	1.28
110. Use test/inventory results for intervention selections	703	3.06	1.24
111. Use aptitude tests	704	2.80	1.37
112. Use achievement tests	705	2.78	1.35
113. Use interest inventories	703	3.11	1.32
114. Use self-report personality inventories	704	3.06	1.23
115. Use intelligence tests	700	2.62	1.29
116. Use nontest appraisal techniques	698	2.73	1.31
117. Engage in needs assessment	698	3.03	1.27
118. Engage in counseling process research	703	1.99	1.11
119. Engage in counseling outcome research	700	2.01	1.12
120. Engage in field/observational research	701	1.87	1.05
121. Engage in experimental/laboratory research	702	1.63	0.91
122. Engage in formative evaluation of counseling program	704	2.45	1.27
123. Engage in summative evaluation of counseling program	700	2.44	1.27
124. Engage in data analyses	699	2.06	1.17
125. Collaborate in research with other professionals	700	2.10	1.16
126. Develop appraisal instrument/technique	701	1.93	1.06
127. Evaluate computer software	695	1.80	1.02
128. Provide expert witness testimony	698	2.41	1.27
129. Participate in professional organization activities	700	2.91	1.30
130. Participate in continuing education/skill enhancement	694	3.55	1.27
131. Write for publication	698	1.98	1.09
132. Write communication for noncounseling, professional activities	698	2.02	1.10
133. Review ethical standards	701	2.84	1.27
134. Supervise counselor trainees	701	2.34	1.30
135. Read current professional literature	701	3.41	1.25
136. Review legal statutes and regulations	702	2.96	1.26
137. Assess programmatic needs	695	2.74	1.27
138. Establish programmatic service goals	700	2.71	1.26
139. Participate in staffing decision-making processes	697	2.87	1.39
140. Allocate financial resources for counseling program	698	2.26	1.27

Item	Number Responding	Mean Rating[a]	(*SD*)
141. Administer counseling program	700	2.57	1.45
142. Use computers for program data management	698	1.99	1.16
143. Conduct fund raising activities for program development/maintenance	696	1.65	0.95
144. Develop program-related reports	698	2.10	1.19
145. Correspond orally with others to maintain communication	695	3.31	1.31
146. Write to other professionals to maintain communication	695	2.79	1.27
147. Evaluate counselors' performance	694	2.74	1.37
148. Provide counselor skill-development training	695	2.63	1.34
149. Serve as liaison with other agencies	691	3.13	1.28
150. Engage in professional/community public relations	698	2.90	1.27
151. Conduct community outreach	695	2.72	1.25
152. Supervise staff	674	2.33	1.39

[a]Response choices: 1 = of no importance, 2 = of little importance, 3 = moderately important, 4 = very important, 5 = critically important.

activities for program development/maintenance (item 143, mean = 1.49), and (e) engage in experimental/laboratory research (item 121, mean = 1.35).

Among the IMPORTANCE data, the five work behaviors having the highest means were (a) use active listening skills (item 34, mean = 4.54), (b) counsel persons in crisis (item 27, mean = 4.40), (c) counsel persons concerning personal change (item 29, mean = 4.19), (d) counsel adults (item 25, mean = 4.09), and (e) assess potential for client to harm self/others (item 5, mean = 4.09). Conversely, the five work behaviors with the lowest level of importance were (a) use computerized "counseling" software (item 18, mean = 1.90), (b) engage in field/observational research (item 120, mean = 1.87), (c) evaluate computer software (item 127, mean = 1.80), (d) conduct fund-raising activities for program development/maintenance (item 143, mean = 1.65), and (e) engage in experimental/laboratory research (item 121, mean = 1.63).

The data resulting from the general ANOVA *F* tests of significance of difference in independent means are presented in Appendix G for the FREQUENCY responses and in Appendix H for the level of IMPORTANCE responses. The p = .01 level of significance was applied for all data analyses. Among the 151 items, relatively few significant differences in either FREQUENCY or IMPORTANCE response means were found on the bases of gender, degree, licensures, or number of certifications held. The greatest numbers of significant differences in both the FREQUENCY and IMPORTANCE response means were accounted for by the difference in job setting. These differences are discussed further in a subsequent subsection of this monograph.

Chapter 4

FACTOR ANALYSES

A primary purpose of the study was to gain understanding of the nature of work behaviors among professional counselors. Factor analysis is a data analysis technique that serves this purpose well. According to Kerlinger (1986):

> Because of its power, elegance, and closeness to the core of scientific purpose, factor analysis can be called the queen of analytic techniques.
>
> Factor analysis serves the cause of scientific parsimony. It tells us, in effect, what . . . measures belong together, which ones measure virtually the same thing, in other words, how much they do so. It thus reduces the number of variables with which the scientist must cope. It also helps the scientist locate and identify unities or fundamental measures. (p. 569)

In general, when applied to data such as those obtained in this study, factor analysis identifies clusters of items (i.e., factors) for which responses are similar. It also facilitates understanding of the nature of the relationships among the clusters. Used within an exploratory perspective, the significant attribute of factor analysis is that it derives clusters of items from actual responses rather than from some theoretical prediction of how items will cluster.

Unfortunately, there are no "hard-and-fast" rules about which type of factor analysis should be used in any particular situation (Amick & Walberg, 1975; Kachigan, 1986; Kerlinger, 1986; Mulaik, 1972). Therefore, several major decisions have to be made in the use of factor analysis as a data analytic technique, including which type of factor analysis procedure (based on type of *communality* estimate) will be used, how many factors will be retained, what will be the minimum factor loading criterion for item retention, and whether an orthogonal or oblique solution is most appropriate.

The term *exploratory* (as opposed to *confirmatory*) factor analysis is used to describe situations in which researchers have little or no basis for hypothesizing about the factor structure of a particular data set. Crocker and Algina (1986) indicated that researchers rarely will have *no* hypothesis about the underlying factor structure prior to analysis, but the term *exploratory factor analysis* remains appropriate if the factor analysis is not intended to confirm a hypothesized factor structure derived from strong theoretical and/or empirical bases. Since no groupings of counselor work behaviors were hypo-thesized before the study, an exploratory factor analysis was used.

The procedure used in this study was a "principal-factors" factor analysis. As Kerlinger (1986) indicated,

> the principal factors method is mathematically satisfying because it yields a mathematically unique solution of a factor problem. Perhaps its major solution feature is that it extracts a maximum amount of variance as each factor is extracted. (p. 576)

One of the primary goals of factor analysis is the achievement of "simple structure" by identifying the minimum number of factors that yield a relatively reasonable and easily interpreted representation of the larger data set (Amick & Walberg, 1975; Harman, 1976; Kerlinger, 1986; Mulaik, 1972). Rules for achieving simple structure have been discussed by numerous authors, but ultimately the nature and degree of achievement of simple structure is determined by the researcher. As Kerlinger (1986) noted,

> a principal factors matrix and its loadings account for the common factor variance of test [or item] scores, but they do not in general provide scientifically meaningful structures. It is the configuration of tests or variables in factor space that are often a fundamental concern. In order to discover these configurations adequately, the arbitrary reference axes must be rotated. (p. 579)

Therefore, a common method for investigating the factor structure of a data set is to conduct a principal-factors factor analysis with an orthogonal transformation using the varimax rotation method and to retain factors having eigenvalues greater than one, known as the Kaiser criterion (Harman, 1976; Karchigan, 1986; Kerlinger, 1986; Mulaik, 1972).

Using the orthogonal solution approach, the initial FREQUENCY responses factor structure contained 10 factors, as shown in Appendix I. Similarly, the initial IMPORTANCE responses factor structure contained 10 factors, as shown in Appendix J. For the FREQUENCY responses, the 10 factors accounted for 53% (80.48/151.00) of the total variance; for the IMPORTANCE responses, the 10 factors accounted for 56% (84.17/151.00) of the total variance.

A common second step in exploring the factor structure of a data set is to conduct a factor analysis with an oblique transformation using the promax rotation method. This step is particularly appropriate when there is no basis for predicting the interfactor correlations and the relationships among factors are unknown. Therefore, this approach also was applied to the FREQUENCY and IMPORTANCE responses. The initial factor structures resulting from an oblique rotation solution to the FREQUENCY and IMPORTANCE response data are shown in Appendices K and L, respectively.

There are no generally agreed-upon methods for estimating the standard errors of factor loadings (Harman, 1976; Kerlinger, 1986), and thus no generally agreed upon criteria for setting the minimum factor loading for retention of items in interpretation of the factor structure. However, Kerlinger (1986) noted that many researchers retain items having factor loadings in the range of .30 to .40. Therefore, based primarily on convention, a criterion level of a factor loading of .40 or higher, which is a relatively "strong" criterion, was used to identify items to be retained for subsequent interpretation of the respective factors. This criterion was deemed appropriate because this investigation focused on an exploration of the *generic* work behaviors of counselors (i.e., those most common to all who identify themselves as counselors).

Identified in each of the initial FREQUENCY and IMPORTANCE orthogonal and oblique solution factor structures to which these criteria were applied were several "unique" factors (see Appendices I, J, K, and L). A unique factor in this context is one in which very few items have factor loadings exceeding the minimum loading criterion; a small number of items account for most of the variance attributable to the unique factor. In general, unique factors within large data sets are undesirable because of the unreliability of measurements based on very few items (Amick & Walberg, 1975; Mulaik, 1972). Therefore, the respective factor analysis procedures were rerun for eight-, seven-, six-, and five-factor solutions. Because the respective eight-, seven-, and six-factor solutions did not present good approximations of simple structure for either the FREQUENCY or IMPORTANCE data sets, a five-factor solution was deemed the most appropriate for both the FREQUENCY and IMPORTANCE data sets.

The complete sets of factor loadings resulting from a five-factor principal factors analysis with orthogonal transformation using varimax rotation for the FREQUENCY and IMPORTANCE responses are shown in Appendices M and N, respectively. For the FREQUENCY responses, the five factors accounted for 41% (61.92/151.00) of the total variance; the five factors for the IMPORTANCE responses accounted for 47% (71.26/151.00) of the total variance.

Shown in Table 4 is the five-factor orthogonal solution for the work behavior statement FREQUENCY responses, with items rank ordered from highest to lowest factor loadings. As is common for a principal-factors analysis of large numbers of variables, some items

Table 4
Five-Factor Orthogonal Solution by Highest Item Loading for the Principal Factors Factor Analysis of FREQUENCY Responses

Factor & loading	Item number	Work behavior
Factor I		
.7112	04	Assess psychosocial needs
.6797	44	Evaluate client's movement toward counseling goals
.6552	06	Clarify client's support systems
.6541	16	Evaluate extent of client's psychological dysfunction
.6296	03	Develop comprehensive treatment plans
.6237	25	Counsel adults
.6164	05	Assess potential for client harm to self/others
.5988	45	Clarify counselor/client role
.5948	31	Counsel clients concerning life-style change
.5860	08	Assist with client's evaluation of counseling
.5841	29	Counsel clients concerning personal change
.5785	07	Systematically observe client behavior
.5704	17	Reframe client's problem
.5660	13	Establish counseling goals

Factor & loading	Item number	Work behavior
.5600	15	Determine DSM-III-R classification
.5499	09	Self-evaluate counseling effectiveness
.5370	46	Clarify client's moral/spiritual issues
.5287	48	Identify client's noncounseling resources
.5279*	76	Counsel concerning marriage enrichment
.5171	14	Analyze cost-benefit of treatment alternatives
.5072	41	Inform client about ethical standards
.5071	43	Evaluate need for client referral
.5053	47	Identify source-of-problem alternatives
.5044	20	Counsel long-term (6 sessions or longer)
.4870	01	Obtain client's informed consent prior to counseling
.4843	42	Inform client about legal aspects of counseling
.4725	32	Counsel clients concerning personality change
.4608	12	Conduct precounseling diagnostic interview
.4530	26	Counsel older persons
.4345	37	Use cognitive-oriented counseling techniques

Factor & loading	Item number	Work behavior
.4298	33	Counsel clients concerning sexual abuse
.4100	40	Inform client about human growth and development
.4081	38	Use brief psychotherapy techniques
Factor II		
.8286	97	Use occupational information
.8217	101	Use print and other media in career counseling
.8098	99	Use career resources library
.7877	113	Use interest inventories
.7549	108	Use test results for client decision making
.7533	50	Provide career/vocational education
.7492	94	Facilitate client's development of job-search skills
.7395	98	Use computerized career counseling resources
.7381	109	Assist client in understanding test results
.6949	95	Provide group vocational counseling
.6936	91	Evaluate client's occupational skills
.6880	111	Use aptitude tests
.6843	104	Provide career counseling for adults

Factor & loading	Item number	Work behavior
.6682	92	Evaluate client's educational preparations
.6657	106	Provide career counseling for persons with dis abilities
.6477	110	Use test/inventory results for intervention selections
.6465	103	Provide career counseling for adolescents
.5951*	107	Select appraisal instruments/techniques for counseling
.5948	105	Provide career counseling for older persons
.5676	112	Use achievement tests
.5533	96	Provide outplacement counseling
.4761	114	Use self-report personality inventories
.4425	127	Evaluate computer software
.4330	18	Use computerized "counseling" software
.4289	93	Facilitate client's development of decision-making skills
Factor III		
.7161	138	Establish programmatic service goals
.7118	137	Assess programmatic needs
.7103	148	Provide counselor skill-development training

Factor & loading	Item number	Work behavior
.6524	147	Evaluate counselors' performance
.6492	144	Develop program-related reports
.6483	125	Collaborate in research with other professionals
.6409	124	Engage in data analyses
.6073	123	Engage in summative evaluation of counseling program
.5977	122	Engage in formative evaluation of counseling program
.5974	150	Engage in professional/community public relations
.5891	126	Develop appraisal instrument/technique
.5864	141	Administer counseling program
.5855	149	Serve as liaison with other agencies
.5756	139	Participate in staffing decision-making processes
.5745	134	Supervise counselor trainees
.5509	151	Conduct community outreach
.5501	152	Supervise staff
.5457	119	Engage in counseling outcome research
.5320	140	Allocate financial resources for counseling program
.5311	120	Engage in field/observationalresearch
.5268	118	Engage in counseling process research
.5256	60	Provide consultation services for human resource needs evaluation
.5237	57	Provide consultation services for organizational development
.5233	58	Provide consultation services for human relation-ships development
.5118	59	Provide consultation services for interpersonal skills training
.5087	62	Provide consultation services for professional skill development
.4804	146	Write to other professionals to maintain communication
.4773	132	Write communication for noncounseling, professional activities
.4721	136	Review legal statutes and regulations
.4477	131	Write for publication
.4472	129	Participate in professional organization activities

Factor & loading	Item number	Work behavior
.4391	61	Provide consultation services for ethical or legal dilemmas
.4295	121	Engage in experimental/laboratory research
.4167	133	Review ethical standards
.4159	142	Use computers for program data management
.4091	55	Provide multicultural training/education
Factor IV		
.8416	82	Evaluate progress toward group goals
.8348	86	Self-evaluate group counseling effectiveness
.8276	84	Assist with group members' feedback to each other
.7885	83	Resolve conflict among group members
.7820	85	Determine group counseling termination criteria
.7772	81	Identify harmful group-member behaviors
.7749	87	Use "structured" activities during group counseling
.7541	80	Systematically observe group members' behaviors
.7348	79	Inform clients of group counseling guidelines and goals

Factor & loading	Item number	Work behavior
.7280	89	Use group-centered group counseling leadership techniques
.7077	88	Use leader-centered group counseling leadership techniques
.4053	90	Use laissez-faire group counseling leadership techniques
Factor V		
.6504*	67	Develop family conflict resolution strategies
.6409*	64	Inform family members of family dynamics
.6341*	66	Clarify family counseling goals
.6322*	69	Use the following family counseling techniques: structural
.6217*	70	Use the following family counseling techniques: strategic
.6112	71	Use the following family counseling techniques: behavioral
.6106*	65	Clarify familial behavior norms
.5899	63	Inform family members of family counseling guidelines and goals
.5846*	68	Use the following family counseling techniques: multigenerational

Factor & loading	Item number	Work behavior
.5739*	78	Counsel concerning family member interaction
.5662*	77	Counsel concerning family change
.4925	23	Counsel children
.4902*	74	Counsel concerning divorce-conflict resolution
.4501	21	Interview client's significant others
.4447*	73	Counsel concerning divorce
.4170*	76	Counsel concerning marriage enrichment

* Factor loadings equal to or greater than .40 on more than one factor.

had factor loadings exceeding the .40 minimum on more than one factor. These items are identified in Table 4 by an asterisk and are listed only once, on the factor for which they have their highest factor loading. The five factors resulting from the orthogonal solution were identified as

I. Fundamental Counseling Practice,
II. Counseling for Career Development,
III. Professional Practice,
IV. Counseling Groups, and
V. Counseling Families.

Table 5 includes the 30 items that did not have a factor loading greater than .40 on any of the five factors. Based on respondents' ratings, these work behaviors were not performed in sufficient frequency to warrant inclusion. The five-factor oblique solution for the FREQUENCY responses is shown in Table 6, with items presented in decreasing order of factor loading. Items having factor loadings equal to or greater than .40 on more than one factor are identified by an asterisk. The factors from the oblique solution were identified as

I. Fundamental Counseling Practice,
II. Counseling for Career Development,
III. Professional Practice,
IV. Counseling Groups, and
V. Counseling Families.

Table 5
Frequency Response Items With Orthogonal Response Factor Loadings of Less Than .40 on Any of the Five Factors

Item Number	Work Behavior
2	Evaluate existing client data
10	Maintain case notes, records, and/or files
11	Conduct former client follow-up activities
19	Counsel short-term (less than 6 sessions)
22	Research use of a specific counseling intervention
24	Counsel adolescents
27	Counsel persons in crisis
28	Counsel clients concerning substance use/abuse
30	Counsel clients concerning physical abuse
34	Use "active listening" skills
35	Use affective-oriented counseling techniques
36	Use behavioral-oriented counseling

Item Number	Work Behavior
36	Use behavioral-oriented counseling techniques
39	Use media resources in counseling
49	Provide human development education
51	Provide mental health enhancement training/education
52	Prepare developmental/preventative media
53	Conduct prevention-oriented developmental activities
54	Conduct self-development training for nonclients
56	Participate in case conferences
72	Counsel concerning premarriage
75	Counsel concerning human sexuality
102	Provide career counseling for children
115	Use intelligence tests
116	Use nontest appraisal techniques
117	Engage in needs assessment
128	Provide expert witness testimony
130	Participate in continuing education/skill enhancement
135	Read current professional literature
143	Conduct fund-raising activities for program development/maintenance
145	Correspond orally with others to maintain communication

The 34 items not having a factor loading equal to or greater than .40 on any of the five factors are presented in Table 7. Based on respondents' ratings, these work behaviors were of insufficient importance to warrant their inclusion.

Table 6

Five-Factor Oblique Solution by Highest Item Loading for the Principal-Factors Factor Analysis of FREQUENCY Responses

Factor & loading	Item number	Work behavior
Factor I		
.7034	25	Counsel adults
.6767	44	Evaluate client's movement toward counseling goals
.6720	04	Assess psychosocial needs
.6401	31	Counsel clients concerning life-style change
.6179	06	Clarify client's support systems
.6115	45	Clarify counselor/client roles
.6034	03	Develop comprehensive treatment plans
.6016	16	Evaluate extent of client's psychological dysfunction
.5726	29	Counsel clients concerning personal change
.5524	13	Establish counseling goals
.5517	08	Assist with client's evaluation of counseling
.5472	09	Self-evaluate counseling effectiveness
.5416	05	Assess potential for client to harm self/others

Factor & loading	Item number	Work behavior
.5389	07	Systematically observe client behaviors
.5320	17	Reframe client's problem
.5186	48	Identify client's noncounseling resources
.5150	43	Evaluate need for client referral
.5111	14	Analyze cost-benefit of treatment alternatives
.5069	26	Counsel older persons
.5046	15	Determine DSM-III-R classification
.4922	41	Inform client about ethical standards and practice
.4823	01	Obtain client's informed consent prior to counseling
.4729	47	Identify source-of-problem alternatives
.4673	42	Inform client about legal aspects of counseling
.4636	46	Clarify client's moral/spiritual issues
.4494	76	Counsel concerning marriage enrichment
.4381	20	Counsel long-term (6 sessions or longer)
.4353	12	Conduct precounseling diagnostic interview
.4133	32	Counsel clients concerning personality change
.4105	37	Use cognitive-oriented counseling techniques
.4024	02	Evaluate existing (precounseling) client data
Factor II		
.8540	97	Use occupational information
.8292	101	Use print and other media in career counseling
.8113	99	Use career resources library
.8012	113	Use interest inventories
.8005	94	Facilitate client's development of job-search skills
.7910	108	Use test results for client decision making
.7831	109	Assist client in understanding test results
.7819	50	Provide career/vocational education
.7454	98	Use computerized career counseling resources
.7372	91	Evaluate client's occupational skills
.7072	111	Use aptitude tests

Factor & loading	Item number	Work behavior
.7058	95	Provide group vocational counseling
.6949	104	Provide career counseling for adults
.6881	92	Evaluate client's educational preparations
.6803	110	Use test/inventory results for intervention selections
.6781	103	Provide career counseling for adolescents
.6725	106	Provide career counseling for persons with disabilities
.6010	105	Provide career counseling for older adults
.5972	107	Select appraisal instruments/techniques for counseling
.5669	112	Use achievement tests
.5520	96	Provide outplacement counseling
.5034	114	Use self-report personality inventories
.4790	93	Facilitate client's development of decision-making skills
.4290	18	Use computerized "counseling" software
Factor III		
.7735	148	Provide counselor skill-development training

Factor & loading	Item number	Work behavior
.7420	138	Establish programmatic service needs
.7341	137	Assess programmatic needs
.7299	147	Evaluate counselors' performance
.6684	144	Develop program-related reports
.6513	125	Collaborate in research with other professionals
.6315	134	Supervise counselor trainees
.6279	124	Engage in data analyses
.6229	152	Supervise staff
.6123	150	Engage in professional/community public relations
.6094	141	Administer counseling program
.6012	139	Participate in staffing decision-making processes
.5999	149	Serve as liaison with other agencies
.5782	151	Conduct community outreach
.5714	126	Develop appraisal instrument/technique
.5661	123	Engage in summative evaluation of counseling program

Factor & loading	Item number	Work behavior
.5555	122	Engage in formative evaluation of counseling program
.5457	140	Allocate financial resources for counseling program
.4994	119	Engage in counseling outcome research
.4975	62	Provide consultation services for professional skill development
.4963	120	Engage in field/observational research
.4926	146	Write to other professionals to maintain communication
.4878	57	Provide consultation services for organizational development
.4861	58	Provide consultation services for human relationships development
.4865	132	Write communication for noncounseling, professional activities
.4851	59	Provide consultation services for interpersonal skills training
.4838	60	Provide consultation services for human resource needs evaluation
.4811	118	Engage in counseling process research
.4905	136	Review legal statutes and regulations
.4747	131	Write for publication
.4268	61	Provide consultation services for ethical or legal dilemmas
.4214	143	Conduct fund-raising activities for program development/maintenance
.4123	129	Participate in professional organization activities
.4060	142	Use computers for program data management
.4018	121	Engage in experimental/laboratory research
Factor IV		
.8670	86	Self-evaluate group counseling effectiveness
.8666	82	Evaluate progress toward group goals
.8567	84	Assist with group members' feedback to each other
.8125	87	Use "structured" activities during group counseling
.8016	83	Resolve conflict among group members
.7962	85	Determine group counseling termination criteria

Factor & loading	Item number	Work behavior
.7940	81	Identify harmful group-member behaviors
.7754	80	Systematically observe group members' behaviors
.7482	79	Inform clients of group counseling guidelines and goals
.7410	89	Use group-centered group counseling leadership techniques
.7266	88	Use leader-centered group counseling leadership techniques
Factor V		
.6735	67	Develop family conflict resolution strategies
.6613	69	Use the following family counseling techniques: structural
.6556	64	Inform family members of family dynamics/roles
.6545	66	Clarify family counseling goals
.6536	70	Use the following family counseling techniques: strategic
.6401	71	Use the following family counseling techniques: behavioral
.6273	65	Clarify familial behavior norms
.6171	68	Use the following family counseling techniques: multigenerational
.6009	63	Inform family members of family counseling guidelines and goals
.5839	78	Counsel concerning family member interaction
.5835	77	Counsel concerning family change
.5262	74	Counsel concerning divorce-conflict resolution
.4929	23	Counsel children
.4633	73	Counsel concerning divorce
.4523	21	Interview client's significant others
.4144	72	Counsel concerning premarriage

Note: All items have factor loadings equal to or greater than .40 on more than one factor

The interfactor correlation matrix for the five-factor oblique solution for FREQUENCY responses is shown in Table 8. Kerlinger (1986) noted that the inter-factor correlations are equivalent to the cosine functions of the angles between factors (i.e., vectors). The data in Table 8 show that the interfactor correlations ranged from .06 to .36. Therefore, the angles between factors ranged from approximately 69° to 88°. Collectively, these data indicate that the factors in the oblique solution are *relatively* uncorrelated. The relative independence in the factors is reflected in the similarity between the five factor orthogonal and oblique solutions for the FREQUENCY responses.

Table 7
Frequency Response Items With Oblique Solution Factor Loadings Less Than .40 on Any of the Five Factors

Item number	Work behavior
10	Maintain case notes, records, and/or files
11	Conduct former client follow-up activities
19	Counsel short-term (less than 6 sessions)
22	Research use of a specific counseling intervention
24	Counsel adolescents
27	Counsel persons in crisis
28	Counsel clients concerning substance use/abuse
30	Counsel clients concerning physical abuse
33	Counsel clients concerning sexual abuse
34	Use "active listening" skills
35	Use affective-oriented counseling techniques
36	Use behavioral-oriented counseling techniques
38	Use brief psychotherapy techniques
39	Use media resources in counseling
40	Inform client about human growth and development
49	Provide human development education
51	Provide mental health enhancement training/education
52	Prepare developmental/preventative media
53	Conduct prevention-oriented developmental activities
54	Conduct self-development training for nonclients
55	Provide multicultural training/education
56	Participate in case conferences
75	Counsel concerning human sexuality
90	Use laissez-faire group counseling leadership techniques
102	Provide career counseling for children
115	Use intelligence tests
116	Use nontest appraisal techniques
117	Engage in needs assessment
127	Evaluate computer software
128	Provide expert witness testimony
130	Participate in continuing education/skill enhancement
133	Review ethical standards
135	Read current professional literature
145	Correspond orally with others to maintain communication

Table 8
Interfactor Correlation Matrix for the Five-Factor Oblique Solution From the Principal-Factors Factor Analysis of FREQUENCY Responses

	Factor				
	1	2	3	4	5
Factor 1	1.0000	-.2112	.0452	.1874	.3056
Factor 2		1.0000	.3590	-.0593	-.1719
Factor 3			1.0000	.2348	.1157
Factor 4				1.0000	.3271
Factor 5					1.0000

Shown in Table 9 is the five-factor orthogonal transformation solution for the IMPORTANCE responses, with the data presented in a manner similar to that for the FREQUENCY responses factor analyses. The five factors of the orthogonal solution for the IMPORTANCE responses were identified as

I. Professional Practice,
II. Counseling for Career Development,
III. Counseling Families,
IV. Fundamental Counseling Practices, and
V. Counseling Groups.

Table 9

Five-Factor Orthogonal Solution by Highest Item Loading for the Principal-Factors Factor Analysis of IMPORTANCE Responses

Factor & loading	Item number	Work behavior
Factor I		
.7574	144	Develop program-related reports
.7502	123	Engage in summative evaluation of counseling program
.7386	125	Collaborate in research with other professionals
.7321	148	Provide counselor skill development training
.7254	122	Engage in formative evaluation of counseling program
.7224	137	Assess programmatic needs
.7223	120	Engage in field/observational research
.7192	134	Supervise counselor trainees
.7173	124	Engage in data analyses
.7116	138	Establish programmatic service goals
.6935	119	Engage in counseling outcome research
.6844	141	Administer counseling program
.6842	139	Participate in staffing decision making processes
.6809	118	Engage in counseling process research
.6777	126	Develop appraisal instrument/technique
.6682	132	Write communication for noncounseling, professional activities
.6630	129	Participate in professional organization activities
.6607	147	Evaluate counselors' performance
.6592	152	Supervise staff
.6574	57	Provide consultation services for organization development
.6545	150	Engage in professional/communitypublic relations
.6511	140	Allocate financial resources for counseling program
.6476	60	Provide consultation services for human resource needs evaluation

Factor & loading	Item number	Work behavior
.6439	62	Provide consultation services for professional skill development
.6367	121	Engage in experimental/laboratory research
.6317	131	Write for publication
.6126	58	Provide consultation services for human relationships development
.6072	59	Provide consultation services for interpersonal skills training
.5996	142	Use computers for program data management
.5911	143	Conduct fund-raising activities for program development/maintenance
.5874	151	Conduct community outreach
.5861	146	Write to other professionals to maintain communication
.5497	61	Provide consultation services for ethical or legal dilemmas
.5325*	127	Evaluate computer software
.5279	130	Participate in continuing education/skill enhancement
.5154	149	Serve as liaison with other agencies
.5107	55	Provide multicultural training/education
.5067*	136	Review legal statutes and regulations
.5036	145	Correspond orally with others to maintain communication
.4915*	135	Read current professional literature

Factor & loading	Item number	Work behavior
.4800	54	Conduct self-development training for nonclients
.4788*	133	Review ethical standards
.4584	52	Prepare developmental/preventative media
.4514	56	Participate in case conferences
.4134	53	Conduct prevention-oriented developmental activities
.4014	102	Provide career counseling for children
Factor II		
.8471	97	Use occupational information
.8251	99	Use career resources library
.8170	101	Use print and other media in career counseling
.8055	91	Evaluate client's occupational skills
.7921	94	Facilitate client's development of job-search skills
.7866	98	Use computerized career counseling resources
.7790	113	Use interest inventories
.7688	95	Provide group vocational counseling
.7649	50	Provide career/vocational education
.7603	92	Evaluate client's educational preparations
.7581	111	Use aptitude tests
.7220	108	Use test results for client decision making

Factor & loading	Item number	Work behavior
.6987	109	Assist client in understanding test results
.6808	106	Provide career counseling for persons with disabilities
.6665	110	Use test/inventory results for intervention selections
.6638	103	Provide career counseling for adolescents
.6445	104	Provide career counseling for adults
.6424	112	Use achievement tests
.6141	96	Provide outplacement counseling
.6097	107	Select appraisal instruments/techniques for counseling
.5654	105	Provide career counseling for older adults
.5572	114	Use self-report personality inventories
.5466	93	Facilitate client's development of decision-making skills
.5070	115	Use intelligence tests
.4563	18	Use computerized "counseling" software
.4556	116	Use nontest appraisal techniques
Factor III		
.7442	67	Develop family conflict resolution strategies
.7396	77	Counsel concerning family change
.7300	74	Counsel concerning divorce-conflict reduction
.7220	78	Counsel concerning family member interaction
.7180	75	Counsel concerning human sexuality
.7049	73	Counsel concerning divorce
.7009	65	Clarify familial behavior norms
.6880	66	Clarify family counseling goals
.6866	64	Inform family members of family dynamics/roles
.6705	69	Use the following family counseling techniques: structural
.6528	76	Counsel concerning marriage enrichment
.6503	70	Use the following family counseling techniques: strategic
.6427	68	Use the following family counseling techniques: multigenerational
.6329	33	Counsel clients concerning sexual abuse
.6249	30	Counsel clients concerning physical abuse
.6175	72	Counsel concerning premarriage
.6080	71	Use the following family counseling techniques: behavioral
.5839	63	Inform family members of family counseling guidelines and goals
.5545	32	Counsel clients concerning personality change
.5129	28	Counsel clients concerning substance use/abuse

Factor & loading	Item number	Work behavior
.4589	23	Counsel children
.4435	46	Clarify client's moral/spiritual issues
.4356	21	Interview client's significant others
.4268	24	Counsel adolescents
.4212	27	Counsel persons in crisis
Factor IV		
.6566	44	Evaluate client's movement toward counseling goals
.6529	13	Establish counseling goals
.6385	09	Self-evaluate counseling effectiveness
.6287	04	Assess psychosocial needs
.6177	07	Systematically observe client behaviors
.6054	08	Assist with client's evaluation of counseling
.5815	16	Evaluate extent of client's psychological dysfunction
.5789	41	Inform client about ethical standards and practice
.5743	02	Evaluate existing (precounseling) client data
.5734	03	Develop comprehensive treatment plans
.5655	45	Clarify counselor/client roles
.5563	43	Evaluate need for client referral
.5517	06	Clarify client's support systems
.5432	01	Obtain client's informed consent prior to counseling

Factor & loading	Item number	Work behavior
.5296	10	Maintain case notes, records, and/or files
.5291	42	Inform client about legal aspects of counseling
.5109	05	Assess potential for client to harm self/others
.4782	12	Conduct precounseling diagnostic interview
.4712	17	Reframe client's problem
.4523	37	Use cognitive-oriented counseling techniques
.4475	14	Analyze cost-benefit of treatment alternatives
.4473	15	Determine DSM-III-R classification
.4365	36	Use behavioral-oriented counseling techniques
.4288	31	Counsel clients concerning life-style change
.4106	47	Identify source-of-problem alternatives
Factor V		
.8166	84	Assist with group members' feedback to each other
.7944	83	Resolve conflict among group members
.7856	82	Evaluate progress toward group goals
.7551	81	Identify harmful group-member behaviors
.7239	87	Use "structured" activities during group counseling

Factor & loading	Item number	Work behavior
.7129	85	Determine group counseling termination criteria
.7128	86	Self-evaluate group counseling effectiveness
.6915	89	Use group-centered group counseling leadership techniques
.6765	88	Use leader-centered group counseling leadership techniques
.6469	79	Inform clients of group counseling guidelines and goals
.6244	80	Systematically observe group members' behaviors

* Factor loadings greater than .40 on more than one factor.

Table 10

IMPORTANCE Response Items With Orthogonal Solution Factor Loadings Less than .40 on Any of the Five Factors

Item number	Work behavior
11	Conduct former client follow-up activities
19	Counsel short-term (less than 6 sessions)
20	Counsel long-term (6 sessions or longer)
22	Research use of a specific counseling intervention
25	Counsel adults
26	Counselor older persons
29	Counsel clients concerning personal change
34	Use "active listening" skills
35	Use affective-oriented counseling techniques
38	Use brief psychotherapy techniques
39	Use media resources in counseling
40	Inform client about human growth and development
48	Identify client's noncounseling resources
49	Provide human development education
51	Provide mental health enhancement training/education
90	Use laissez-faire group counseling leadership techniques
117	Engage in needs assessment
128	Provide expert witness testimony

Eighteen items did not have a factor loading of .40 or greater on any of the factors. These are presented in Table 10. The five factor oblique solution for IMPORTANCE responses is shown in Table 11. The factors also were identified as

I. Professional Practice,
II. Counseling for Career Development,
III. Counseling Families,
IV. Fundamental Counseling Practices, and
V. Counseling Groups.

Table 11

Five-Factor Oblique Solution by Highest Item Loading for the Principal-Factors Factor Analysis of IMPORTANCE Responses

Factor & loading	Item number	Work behavior
Factor I		
.8086	144	Develop program-related reports
.7870	125	Collaborate in research with other professionals
.7818	148	Provide counselor skill-development training

Factor & loading	Item number	Work behavior
.7754	123	Engage in summative evaluation of counseling program
.7701	134	Supervise counselor trainees
.7516	124	Engage in data analyses
.7445	120	Engage in field/observational research
.7425	137	Assess programmatic needs
.7409	122	Engage in formative evaluation of counseling program
.7293	141	Administer counseling program
.7270	138	Establish programmatic service goals
.7231	139	Participate in staffing decision making processes
.7210	152	Supervise staff
.7100	132	Write communication for noncounseling, professional activities
.6915	119	Engage in counseling outcome research
.6862	147	Evaluate counselors' performance
.6854	126	Develop appraisal instrument/techniques
.6839	150	Engage in professional/community public relations
.6770	118	Engage in counseling process research
.6723	131	Write for publication
.6702	57	Provide consultation services for organizational development
.6658	140	Allocate financial resources for counseling program
.6587	129	Participate in professional organization activities
.6539	60	Provide consultation services for human resource needs evaluation
.6483	62	Provide consultation services for professional skill development
.6404	121	Engage in experimental/laboratory research
.6306	143	Conduct fund-raising activities for program development/maintenance
.6124	142	Use computers for program data management
.6122	146	Write to other professionals to maintain communication
.6062	151	Conduct community outreach
.6034	58	Provide consultation services for human relationships development
.6006	59	Provide consultation services for interpersonal skills training
.5611	61	Provide consultation services for ethical or legal dilemmas
.5249	149	Serve as liaison with other agencies
.5093	130	Participate in continuing education/skill enhancement
.5064	145	Correspond orally with others to maintain communication
.4871	55	Provide multicultural training/education

Factor & loading	Item number	Work behavior
.4793	127	Evaluate computer software
.4742	136	Review legal statutes and regulations
.4707	135	Read current professional literature
.4692	54	Conduct self-development training for nonclients
.4482	133	Review ethical standards
.4224	52	Prepare developmental/preventative media
.4101	56	Participate in case conferences
Factor II		
.8634	97	Use occupational information
.8366	91	Evaluate client's occupational skills
.8287	99	Use career resources library
.8255	101	Use print and other media in career counseling
.8211	94	Facilitate client's development of job-search skills
.8064	98	Use computerized career counseling resources
.7951	113	Use interest inventories
.7948	50	Provide career/vocational education
.7827	92	Evaluate client's educational preparations
.7748	111	Use aptitude tests
.7739	95	Provide group vocational counseling

Factor & loading	Item number	Work behavior
.7291	109	Assist client in understanding test results
.7236	108	Use test results for client decision making
.6924	103	Provide career counseling for adolescents
.6646	110	Use test/inventory results for intervention selections
.6630	106	Provide career counseling for persons with disabilities
.6361	104	Provide career counseling for adults
.6335	112	Use achievement tests
.5943	93	Facilitate client's development of decision making skills
.5845	96	Provide outplacement counseling
.5701	107	Select appraisal instruments/techniques for counseling
.5680	114	Use self-report personality inventories
.5303	105	Provide career counseling for older adults
.5112	115	Use intelligence tests
.4294	18	Use computerized "counseling" software
.4148	116	Use nontest appraisal techniques
Factor III		
.7894	74	Counsel concerning divorce-conflict resolution
.7695	75	Counsel concerning human sexuality

Factor & loading	Item number	Work behavior
.7620	73	Counsel concerning divorce
.7553	77	Counsel concerning family change
.7534	67	Develop family conflict resolution strategies
.7252	78	Counsel concerning family member interaction
.6852	65	Clarify familial behavior norms
.6684	72	Counsel concerning premarriage
.6645	66	Clarify family counseling goals
.6586	64	Inform family of family dynamics/roles
.6568	69	Use the following family counseling techniques: structural
.6399	68	Use the following family counseling techniques: multigenerational
.6374	70	Use the following family counseling techniques: strategic
.6245	33	Counsel clients concerning sexual abuse
.6105	30	Counsel clients concerning physical abuse
.5965	71	Use the following family counseling techniques: behavioral
.5492	32	Counsel clients concerning personality change
.5214	63	Inform family members of family counseling guidelines and goals

Factor & loading	Item number	Work behavior
.5146	28	Counsel clients concerning substance use/abuse
.4494	76	Counsel concerning marriage enrichment
.4296	24	Counsel adolescents
.4929	23	Counsel children
Factor IV		
.6774	44	Evaluate client's movement toward counseling goals
.6753	13	Establish counseling goals
.6511	09	Self-evaluate counseling effectiveness
.6337	04	Assess psychosocial needs
.6181	08	Assist with client's evaluation of counseling
.6124	07	Systematically observe client behaviors
.6104	02	Evaluate existing (precounseling) client data
.5730	41	Inform client about ethical standards and practice
.5693	45	Clarify counselor/client roles
.5650	03	Develop comprehensive treatment plans
.5650	01	Obtain client's informed consent prior to counseling
.5604	43	Evaluate need for client referral
.5572	16	Evaluate extent of client's psychological dysfunction
.5517	10	Maintain case notes, records, and/or files
.5393	06	Clarify client's support systems

Factor & loading	Item number	Work behavior
.5227	42	Inform client about legal aspects of counseling
.4770	05	Assess potential for client to harm self/others
.4649	17	Reframe client's problem
.4591	12	Conduct precounseling diagnostic interview
.4466	14	Analyze cost-benefit of treatment alternatives
.4274	37	Use cognitive-oriented counseling techniques
.4152	31	Counsel clients concerning life-style change
.4086	36	Use behavioral-oriented counseling techniques
.4039	15	Determine DSM-III-R classification
Factor V		
.8546	84	Assist with group members' feedback to each other
.8334	83	Resolve conflict among group members
.8110	82	Evaluate progress toward group goals
.7765	87	Use "structured" activities during group counseling
.7720	81	Identify harmful group-member behaviors
.7262	86	Self-evaluate group counseling effectiveness
.7254	85	Determine group counseling termination criteria
.7131	88	Use leader-centered group counseling leadership techniques
.7105	89	Use group-centered group counseling leadership techniques
.6487	79	Inform clients of group counseling guidelines and goals
.6155	80	Systematically observe group members' behaviors

* Note: All items have factor loadings equal to or greater than .40 on more than one factor.

Twenty-three items did not have factor loadings of .40 or greater on any of the five factors. They are presented in Table 12. The interfactor correlation matrix for the five-factor oblique transformation solution for IMPORTANCE responses is shown in Table 13. The interfactor correlations ranged from approximately .02 to .42, and, therefore, the angles between factors ranged from approximately 66° to 89°. Thus, the factors in the oblique solution for IMPORTANCE responses also are *relatively* uncorrelated.

Table 12
IMPORTANCE Response Items With Oblique Solution Factor Loadings Less Than .40 on Any of the Five Factors

Item number	Work behavior
11	Conduct former client follow-up activities
19	Counsel short-term (less than 6 sessions)
20	Counsel long-term (6 sessions or longer)
21	Interview client's significant others
22	Research use of a specific counseling intervention
25	Counsel adults
26	Counsel older persons

Item number	Work behavior
27	Counsel persons in crisis
29	Counsel clients concerning personal change
34	Use "active listening" skills
35	Use affective-oriented counseling techniques
38	Use brief psychotherapy techniques
39	Use media resources in counseling
40	Inform client about human growth and development
46	Clarify client's moral/spiritual issues
47	Identify source-of-problem alternatives
48	Identify client's noncounseling resources
49	Provide human development education
51	Provide mental health enhancement training/education
53	Conduct prevention-oriented developmental activities
90	Use laissez-faire group counseling leadership techniques
102	Provide career counseling for children
117	Engage in needs assessment
128	Provide expert witness testimony

Table 13
Interfactor Correlation Matrix for the Five Factor Oblique Solution From the Principal Factors Factor Analysis of IMPORTANCE Responses

	Factor				
	1	2	3	4	5
Factor 1	1.0000	.4235	.2353	.3942	.2649
Factor 2		1.0000	-.0822	.0930	-.0196
Factor 3			1.0000	.4163	.4097
Factor 4				1.0000	.2922
Factor 5					1.0000

The decision to focus on an oblique or an orthogonal transformation solution for the factor analysis of a data set ultimately is up to the researcher(s) because there are no established rules for making the decision (Kerlinger, 1986). In general, an oblique solution is considered to approximate an orthogonal solution when the angles between factors are "relatively large," often interpreted to mean greater than 45°. The angles between factors in the oblique transformation solutions here for both the FREQUENCY and IMPORTANCE responses are indeed relatively large. This means that respondents distinguished relatively clearly among their patterns of responses to the respective clusters of both FREQUENCY and IMPORTANCE items. Therefore, the discussion that follows focuses on the orthogonal transformation solutions for both the FREQUENCY and IMPORTANCE responses.

A high *internal* congruence exists within the respective FREQUENCY and IMPORTANCE responses of the orthogonal transformation factor structures. That is, within each of the factor structures, very few items seem "out of place" on the factors relative to the factor names. Equally important is the similarity between the two factor structures, as reflected in the same five factor names being applicable to both factor structures although the order of the named factors differs in the two structures.

A major purpose of this study was to develop a list of work behaviors that effectively characterizes the work of those who describe themselves as professional counselors. The respective factor analyses facilitate development of this list through identification of coherent clusters of work behaviors; at least the items that load heavily (i.e., greater than .40) on the respective factors should be retained. Attention, however, also should be given to those items that did not load heavily on any of the factors. In this regard, IMPORTANCE data are of more significance than FREQUENCY data because items deemed important for successful professional practice should be included even if they are used with low or widely varying frequency by professional counselors.

Examination of the means (see Table 3) for the 18 items not loading at the criterion level on any of the five factors in the orthogonal solution for IMPORTANCE responses (see Table 9) reveals that three items had means greater than 4.00, which is a reasonable criterion for "very important." Item 25 (Counsel adults) had a mean of 4.09 and item 29 (Counsel clients concerning personal change) a mean of 4.19 for the IMPORTANCE ratings. Both item 25 and item 29 had their highest factor loadings, .3657 and .3668, respectively, on Factor IV, Fundamental Counseling Practices, in the orthogonal solution for IMPORTANCE responses. These loadings are close to the minimum factor loading criterion used. Coincidentally, these items had their highest factor loadings, .6237 and .5841, respectively, on Factor I, Fundamental Counseling Practices, in the orthogonal solution for the FREQUENCY responses. Therefore, these items were added to the set for that factor.

Item 34 (Use "active listening" skills) is an item apparently unique within the set. It had the highest FREQUENCY response mean (4.77), as well as the highest IMPORTANCE response mean (4.54). It also emerged as a unique factor in each of the factor analyses. Quite obviously, use of active listening skills is a frequent and important counseling behavior. It appears to be one that underlies much of what is done by professional counselors, and it may be a "universal" counseling behavior. Therefore, because of its significance, it too should be added to the list. Because of its uniqueness as a factor and its universality as a counseling behavior, item 34 could be added to any of the factors. However, perhaps its most appropriate placement for purposes here is in Factor IV, Fundamental Counseling Practices.

The overall result of the factor analyses is a set of 136 work behaviors that can be subdivided into five relatively distinct subsets of counselor functions, each of which includes relatively consistent ratings of frequency and importance of work behaviors. Therefore, subsequent analyses and interpretations should be made in regard to this set of items.

Chapter 5

FURTHER ANALYSES

Using the data presented in Table 2, it is possible to determine the *relative* differences in work behavior frequencies among the five clusters encompassing the 136 work behaviors by computing the mean item means within the respective clusters. Ordered from highest to lowest, the means of the work behavior cluster FREQUENCY item means were as follows: Fundamental Counseling Practices, 3.89 (28 items); Counseling Groups, 3.30 (11 items); Counseling Families, 2.92 (25 items); Counseling for Career Development, 2.76 (26 items); and Professional Practice, 2.67 (46 items). In general, the responding counselors engaged in fundamental counseling practices and counseling groups with relatively greater frequency than they engaged in counseling families, counseling for career development, and professional practices. Although differences among these means could be determined, the statistical significance of those differences is not of particular importance here. Intuitively, the pattern of differences is in accord with common perceptions of counselors' patterns of work behaviors. Counselors spend (a) most of their time engaged in fundamental counseling behaviors such as those for individual counseling and/or applicable to all types of counseling, (b) somewhat less time in counseling groups, and (c) the least amount of time in specialized activities such as counseling families, counseling for career development, and professional practice activities.

Interpretation of the data presented in Appendix G (i.e., ANOVAs for FREQUENCY responses data) can be used to facilitate understanding of how counselors having different characteristics and/or employment situations engaged in the 136 work behaviors. Shown in Table 14 are numbers of larger FREQUENCY means by demographic characteristics for the various clusters. For example, Fundamental Counseling Practice frequencies included only one statistically significant difference on the basis of gender (with females having the higher mean), degree level (with doctoral level counselors having the higher mean), and licensures held (with licensed professional counselors having the higher mean) and two statistically significant differences on the basis of certifications held (with counselors holding only NCC certification having the higher mean). However, there were 22 statistically significant differences on the basis of employment setting, with counselors in community settings having higher means than counselors in academic/educational settings for 17 of the 22 differences. A similar pattern was found for items in the Counseling Families cluster.

Table 14
Numbers of Larger Means by Respondent Demographic Characteristics for Significant Differences in FREQUENCY Item Means for the Five Work Behavior Clusters

Cluster	Number of Larger Means: Gender		Degree Level		Job Setting		Licensures		Certifications	
	F	M	DL	EL	ED	CM	PC	OL	NC	OC
Fundamental Counseling Practices (28 items)	1		1		5	17	1		2	
Counseling Groups (11 items)					1					
Counseling Families (25 items)	2		4		4	18		1		1
Counseling for Career Development (26 items)			1		18			3		5
Professional Practices (46 items)	1	4	1	15	30	1		1	2	2

Note: M = male; F = female; DL = doctoral level; EL = entry level; ED = educational; CM = community; PC = professional counselor; OL = other licensures; NC = NCC only; OC = other certifications.

There was only one significant difference among items in the Counseling Groups category. The most evident trend in the Counseling for Career Development and Professional Practices clusters was that counselors in academic/educational settings reported significantly higher frequencies for most of the items in those clusters. Therefore, the greatest variation in the frequencies in which counselors engaged in the various work behaviors concerned employment in a community or academic/educational setting.

Similar analyses and interpretations can be made for the IMPORTANCE responses data. The order of means of the IMPORTANCE items means within the five clusters of work behaviors was as follows: Fundamental Counseling Practices, 3.65 (28 items); Counseling Groups, 3.36 (11 items); Counseling Families, 3.26 (25 items); Counseling for Career Development, 2.89 (26 items); and Professional Practices, 2.48 (46 items). The *order* of differences among these means is the same as that for the FREQUENCY data. However, the pattern of differences is less distinct. Even though the respondents apparently engage in counseling groups relatively more frequently than they engage in counseling families, they ascribe relatively equal importance to the respective sets of work behaviors. Also, the res-pondents appear to place much less importance on professional practice activities than they do on their fundamental, group, or family counseling activities.

Interpretation of the data presented in Appendix H (i.e., ANOVAs of IMPORTANCE responses data) can be used to facilitate understanding of the relative importance counselors ascribed to the clusters of work behaviors. Shown in Table 15 are the number of larger IMPORTANCE means by respondent demographic characteristics for the five work behavior clusters. It is evident that there are far fewer significant differences in the IMPORTANCE means than there were among the FREQUENCY means. An additional obvious point among the data in Table 15 is that counselors employed in academic/educational settings place greater importance on counseling for career development activities than do counselors employed in community settings.

Table 15
Numbers of Larger Means By Respondent Demographic Characteristics for Significant Differences in IMPORTANCE Item Means for the Five Work Behavior Clusters

Number of Larger Means

Cluster	Gender		Degree Level		Job Setting		Licensures		Certifications	
	F	M	DL	EL	ED	CM	PC	OL	NC	OC
Fundamental Counseling Practices (28 items)	1		1	1	4	9		1	1	
Counseling Groups (11 items)					1					
Counseling Families (25 items)		1		2	1	6				1
Counseling for Career Development (26 items)		5			21		1			6
Professional Practices (46 items)		6	2	1	18		1		1	5

Note: M = male; F = Female; DL = doctoral level; EL = entry level; ED = educational; CM = Community; PC = professional counselor; NC = NCC only; OC = other certifications.

Prioritizations

The data resulting from the independent analyses of the FREQUENCY and IMPORTANCE responses are extremely enlightening and useful. However, combining the data has the potential to be of even greater utilitarian value because independent considerations may not accurately portray the overall situation. For example, some work behaviors may be performed relatively frequently but may not be viewed as having great importance to successful and effective professional counseling. Conversely, some work behaviors judged to be very important to successful and effective professional counseling may be performed relatively infrequently. Therefore, it is desirable to "combine" the FREQUENCY and IMPORTANCE data to yield a hierarchy of "combined" judgments or weightings about the work behaviors of professional counselors.

Kane, et al. (1989) provided an overview of methods used to combine job analysis frequency and importance data such as those derived in this study. They categorized potential combined weighting strategies as either *additive* or *multiplicative* methods. For the additive model, the FREQUENCY and IMPORTANCE item response means would be added, and then the items would be prioritized by the respective item mean sums. Although this model is mathematically simple, its results are not easily understood.

The advantages and interpretations of the application of a multiplicative method were summarized by Kane et al. (1989):

> A multiplicative model is more statistically complicated . . . but makes more sense. We can think of criticality [combined index value (CIV)] of an activity as a measure of the consequences that may result from the activity, on the average, each time the activity is performed. ... The overall importance [CIV] of the activity for practice then could be estimated by summing criticality [IMPORTANCE] over all occurrences or, more simply, by multiplying the criticality [IMPORTANCE] by the frequency. (p. 19)

Based on the potential relative values of the results of applications of each of the methods, a multiplicative method was applied to the data from this study.

A key decision in the application of a multiplicative method is determination of the so-called *effective* contribution or weight of each of the variables. That is, should FREQUENCY and IMPORTANCE data be given equal or differentiated (i.e., weighted) values in the multiplicative process? It might be argued that, in a job analysis, frequency of activity should be given greater effective weighting because it reflects actual (as opposed to relatively valued) activities (i.e., work behaviors). However, according to Kane et al. (1989):

> The relative emphasis that should be given to frequency and criticality [IMPORTANCE] in determining importance [CIV] is a matter of judgment. However, for licensure [or certification] that is intended to protect the public from harm or unnecessary risk, criticality [IMPORTANCE] would seem to be of at least as much concern as frequency.
>
> Activities that are critical [important] in the sense that their omission or inadequate performance would pose substantial risk to clients are directly related to the purposes of licensure [or certification], even if they have relatively low frequency. By contrast, activities that are performed frequently but have very low criticality [IMPORTANCE] would be less important for protection of the public than their frequency might suggest. (p. 20)

Therefore, following the comments and example of Kane et al. (1989), the effective weights of FREQUENCY and IMPORTANCE were considered to be equal in this study. In essence, the use of equal effective means that the item CIVs computed will not be distorted by *extreme* item

FREQUENCY or IMPORTANCE ratings.

The full set of computations leading to application of the multiplicative method used in this study is too extensive to be presented here; interested readers are referred to Kane et al. (1989) for the formulas applied. However, the results recommended by the application of the multiplicative method (using adjusted weightings, as recommended by Kane et al.) are of interest.

Presented in Table 16 are the item CIVs, which are rank ordered within the five clusters of work behaviors. Within the Professional Practice cluster, items related to professional interactions had the highest weightings. Items related to use of tests, particularly in regard to facilitating client decision making, had the highest weightings within the Counseling for Career Development Cluster. Counseling persons in crisis was the preeminent item in the Counseling Families cluster. Items related to what are generally considered to be crucial parts of counseling processes, such as establishing goals and assessing client progress in counseling, had the highest weightings in the Fundamental Counseling Practices cluster. Similarly, facilitating group members' individual and collective progress through group counseling was reflected in the highest item weightings in the Counseling Groups cluster.

Table 16

Work Behavior Item Combined Index Values Rank-Ordered by Adjusted Weight Within Cluster Areas

Factor & combined index value	Item number	Work behavior
Factor I: Professional Practice		
.00705	149	Serve as liaison with other agencies
.00670	61	Provide consultation services for ethical or legal dilemmas
.00649	56	Participate in case conferences
.00642	141	Administer counseling program
.00638	53	Conduct prevention-oriented developmental activities
.00623	139	Participate in staffing decision-making processes
.00576	150	Engage in professional/community public relations
.00566	130	Participate in continuing education/skill enhancement
.00562	151	Conduct community outreach
.00558	145	Correspond orally with others to maintain communication
.00553	147	Evaluate counselors' performance

Factor & combined index value	Item number	Work behavior
.00553	138	Establish programmatic service goals
.00541	135	Read current professional literature
.00536	146	Write to other professionals to maintain communication
.00519	129	Participate in professional organization activities
.00516	137	Assess programmatic needs
.00511	136	Review legal statutes and regulations
.00511	152	Supervise staff
.00506	148	Provide counselor skill-development training
.00502	133	Review ethical standards
.00492	59	Provide consultation services for interpersonal skills training
.00470	58	Provide consultation services for human relationships development
.00466	60	Provide consultation services for human resource needs evaluation
.00462	122	Engage in formative evaluation of counseling program
.00461	123	Engage in summative evaluation of counseling program
.00449	134	Supervise counselor trainees

Factor & combined index value	Item number	Work behavior
.00448	62	Provide consultation services for professional skill development
.00435	52	Prepare devel- opmental/preventative media
.00434	144	Develop program-related reports
.00433	140	Allocate financial resources for counseling program
.00428	54	Conduct self-development training for nonclients
.00424	57	Provide consultation services for organizational development
.00421	55	Provide multicultural training/education
.00380	142	Use computers for program data management
.00356	124	Engage in data analyses
.00355	132	Write communication for noncounseling, professional activities
.00329	125	Collaborate in research with other professionals
.00289	119	Engage in counseling outcome research
.00289	118	Engage in counseling process research
.00282	131	Write for publication
.00278	102	Provide career counseling for children

Factor & combined index value	Item number	Work behavior
.00270	126	Develop appraisal instrument/technique
.00249	120	Engage in field/observational research
.00219	127	Evaluate computer software
.00173	143	Conduct fund-raising activities for program development/maintenance
.00140	121	Engage in experi-mental/laboratory research
Factor II: Counseling for Career Development		
.01010	109	Assist client in understanding test results
.00916	93	Facilitate client's development of decision-making skills
.00796	108	Use test results for client decision making
.00772	113	Use interest inventories
.00765	92	Evaluate client's educational preparations
.00725	114	Use self-report personality inventories
.00700	110	Use test/inventory results for intervention selections
.00691	91	Evaluate client's occupational skills
.00687	97	Use occupational information
.00684	50	Provide career/vocational education

Factor & combined index value	Item number	Work behavior
.00667	94	Facilitate client's development of job-search skills
.00664	112	Use achievement tests
.00626	103	Provide career counseling for adolescents
.00624	101	Use print and other media in career counseling
.00623	107	Select appraisal instruments/techniques for counseling
.00622	104	Provide career counseling for adults
.00609	116	Use non-test appraisal techniques
.00608	111	Use aptitude tests
.00571	99	Use career resources library
.00516	115	Use intelligence tests
.00509	98	Use computerized career counseling resources
.00482	106	Provide career counseling for persons with disabilities
.00474	95	Provide group vocational counseling
.00407	105	Provide career counseling for older adults
.00363	96	Provide outplacement counseling
.00296	18	Use computerized "counseling" software

Factor & combined index value	Item number	Work behavior
Factor III: Counseling Families		
.01224	27	Counsel persons in crisis
.00942	28	Counsel clients concerning substance use/abuse
.00933	33	Counsel clients concerning sexual abuse
.00928	24	Counsel adolescents
.00924	78	Counsel concerning family member interaction
.00895	32	Counsel clients concerning personality change
.00890	30	Counsel clients concerning physical abuse
.00870	67	Develop family conflict-resolution strategies
.00851	77	Counsel concerning family change
.00799	66	Clarify family counseling goals
.00787	65	Clarify familial behavior norms
.00776	64	Inform family members of family dynamics/roles
.00761	63	Inform family members of family counseling guidelines and goals
.00695	46	Clarify client's moral/spiritual issues
.00667	73	Counsel concerning divorce
.00644	23	Counsel children
.00640	75	Counsel concerning human sexuality
.00611	74	Counsel concerning divorce-conflict reduction
.00578	21	Interview client's significant others
.00554	71	Use the following family counseling techniques: behavioral
.00502	76	Counsel concerning marriage enrichment
.00486	69	Use the following family counseling techniques: structural
.00468	70	Use the following family counseling techniques: strategic
.00459	68	Use the following family counseling techniques: multigenerational
.00364	72	Counsel concerning premarriage
Factor IV: Fundamental Counseling Practices		
.01305	29	Counsel clients concerning personal change
.01287	13	Establish counseling goals
.01100	05	Assess potential for client to harm self/others
.01077	44	Evaluate client's movement toward counseling goals

Factor & combined index value	Item number	Work behavior
.01065	16	Evaluate extent of client's psychological dysfunction
.01061	25	Counsel adults
.01028	45	Clarify counselor/client roles
.01028	03	Develop comprehensive treatment plans
.01007	08	Assist with client's evaluation of counseling
.01003	17	Reframe client's problem
.00990	47	Identify source-of-problem alternatives
.00975	01	Obtain client's informed consent prior to counseling
.00964	31	Counsel clients concerning life-style change
.00964	41	Inform client about ethical standards and practice
.00951	06	Clarify client's support systems
.00929	04	Assess psychosocial needs
.00906	07	Systematically observe client behaviors
.00876	43	Evaluate need for client referral
.00838	02	Evaluate existing (precounseling) client data
.00819	12	Conduct precounseling diagnostic interview
.00788	34	Use "active listening" skills
.00731	10	Maintain case notes, records, and/or files
.00728	37	Use cognitive-oriented counseling techniques
.00727	9	Self-evaluate counseling effectiveness
.00689	42	Inform client about legal aspects of counseling
.00679	36	Use behavioral-oriented counseling techniques
.00563	15	Determine DSM-III-R classification
.00561	14	Analyze cost-benefit of treatment alternatives
Factor V: Counseling Groups		
.01056	84	Assist with group members' feedback to each other
.01018	81	Identify harmful group-member behaviors
.01012	82	Evaluate progress toward group goals
.00969	83	Resolve conflict among group members
.00956	86	Self-evaluate group counseling effectiveness
.00912	85	Determine group counseling termination criteria
.00889	79	Inform clients of group counseling guidelines and goals

Factor & combined index value	Item number	Work behavior
.00862	80	Systematically observe group members' behaviors
.00818	87	Use "structured" activities during group counseling
.00759	89	Use group-centered group counseling leadership techniques
.00680	88	Use leader-centered group counseling leadership techniques

In general, the items within the respective clusters having the highest weightings were those that focused on counselors working with others in a variety of ways to facilitate counseling effectiveness. Items having relatively lower weightings within the clusters tended to be those that focused on relatively specific ways of behaving (e.g., using a particular counseling approach or technique).

Shown in Table 17 are the same items rank ordered by adjusted weights across the full set of 136 work behaviors. As with the unadjusted mean data, items having the highest weightings are those related to helping clients progress through counseling effectively, irrespective of the particular counseling processes used. Clearly, the professional counselor respondents in this study most frequently engaged in direct counseling processes and valued those activities over other professional activities. Conversely, activities that may be considered tangential to direct provision of counseling services had the lowest weightings. However, it should be remembered that the work behaviors presented in Tables 16 and 17 are those determined to be common among professional counselors, and, therefore, those receiving low weightings in the lists are significant within the broader context of the counseling profession.

Table 17
Work Behavior Item Combined Index Values Rank Ordered by Adjusted Weight

Combined index value	Item number	Work behavior
.01305	29	Counsel clients concerning personal change
.01287	13	Establish counseling goals
.01224	27	Counsel persons in crisis
.01100	05	Assess potential for client to harm self/others
.01077	44	Evaluate client's movement toward counseling goals
.01065	16	Evaluate extent of client's psychological dysfunction
.01061	25	Counsel adults

Combined index value	Item number	Work behavior
.01056	84	Assist with group members' feedback to each other
.01028	45	Clarify counselor/client roles
.01028	03	Develop comprehensive treatment plans
.01018	81	Identify harmful group-member behaviors
.01012	82	Evaluate progress toward group goals
.01010	109	Assist client in understanding test results
.01007	08	Assist with client's evaluation of counseling
.01003	17	Reframe client's problem
.00990	47	Identify source-of-problem alternatives
.00975	01	Obtain client's informed consent prior to counseling
.00969	83	Resolve conflict among group members
.00964	31	Counsel clients concerning life-style change
.00964	41	Inform client about ethical standards and practice
.00956	86	Self-evaluate group counseling effectiveness
.00951	06	Clarify client's support systems
.00942	28	Counsel clients concerning substance use/abuse
.00933	33	Counsel clients concerning sexual abuse
.00929	04	Assess psychosocial needs
.00928	24	Counsel adolescents

Combined index value	Item number	Work behavior
.00924	78	Counsel concerning family member interaction
.00916	93	Facilitate client's development of decision-making skills
.00912	85	Determine group counseling termination criteria
.00906	07	Systematically observe client behaviors
.00895	32	Counsel clients concerning personality change
.00890	30	Counsel clients concerning physical abuse
.00889	79	Inform clients of group counseling guidelines and goals
.00876	43	Evaluate need for client referral
.00870	67	Develop family conflict resolution strategies
.00862	80	Systematically observe group members' behaviors
.00851	77	Counsel concerning family change
.00838	02	Evaluate existing (precounseling client data
.00819	12	Conduct precounseling diagnostic interview
.00818	87	Use "structured" activities during group counseling
.00799	66	Clarify family counseling goals
.00796	108	Use test results for client decision making
.00788	34	Use "active listening" skills
.00787	65	Clarify familial behavior norms

Combined index value	Item number	Work behavior
.00776	64	Inform family members of family dynamics/roles
.00772	113	Use interest inventories
.00765	92	Evaluate client's educational preparations
.00761	63	Inform family members of family counseling guidelines and goals
.00759	89	Use group-centered group counseling leadership techniques
.00731	10	Maintain case notes, records, and/or files
.00728	37	Use cognitive-oriented counseling techniques
.00727	09	Self-evaluate counseling effectiveness
.00725	114	Use self-report personality inventories
.00705	149	Serve as liaison with other agencies
.00700	110	Use test/inventory results for intervention selections
.00695	46	Clarify client's moral/spiritual issues
.00691	91	Evaluate client's occupational skills
.00689	42	Inform client about legal aspects of counseling
.00687	97	Use occupational information
.00684	50	Provide career/vocational education
.00680	88	Use leader-centered group counseling leadership techniques
.00679	36	Use behavioral-oriented counseling techniques

Combined index value	Item number	Work behavior
.00670	61	Provide consultation services for ethical or legal dilemmas
.00667	73	Counsel concerning divorce
.00667	94	Facilitate client's development of job-search skills
.00664	112	Use achievement tests
.00649	56	Participate in case conferences
.00644	23	Counsel children
.00642	141	Administer counseling program
.00640	75	Counsel concerning human sexuality
.00638	53	Conduct prevention-oriented developmental activities
.00626	103	Provide career counseling for adolescents
.00624	101	Use print and other media in career counseling
.00623	139	Participate in staffing decision-making processes
.00623	107	Select appraisal instruments/techniques for counseling
.00622	104	Provide career counseling for adults
.00611	74	Counsel concerning divorce-conflict reduction
.00609	116	Use nontest appraisal techniques
.00608	111	Use aptitude tests
.00578	21	Interview client's significant others

Combined index value	Item number	Work behavior
.00576	150	Engage in professional/community public relations
.00571	99	Use career resources library
.00566	130	Participate in continuing education/skill enhancement
.00563	15	Determine DSM-III-R classification
.00562	151	Conduct community outreach
.00561	14	Analyze cost-benefit of treatment alternatives
.00558	145	Correspond orally with others to maintain communication
.00554	71	Use the following family counseling techniques: behavioral
.00553	147	Evaluate counselors' performance
.00553	138	Establish programmatic service goals
.00541	135	Read current professional literature
.00536	146	Write to other professionals to maintain communication
.00519	129	Participate in professional organization activities
.00516	137	Assess programmatic needs
.00516	115	Use intelligence tests
.00511	136	Review legal statutes and regulations
.00511	152	Supervise staff
.00509	98	Use computerized career counseling resources

Combined index value	Item number	Work behavior
.00506	148	Provide counselor skill-development training
.00502	133	Review ethical standards
.00502	76	Counsel concerning marriage enrichment
.00492	59	Provide consultation services for interpersonal skills training
.00486	69	Use the following family counseling techniques: structural
.00482	106	Provide career counseling for persons with disabilities
.00474	95	Provide group vocational counseling
.00470	58	Provide consultation services for human relationships development
.00468	70	Use the following family counseling techniques: strategic
.00466	60	Provide consultation services for human resource needs evaluation
.00462	122	Engage in formative evaluation of counseling program
.00461	123	Engage in summative evaluation of counseling program
.00459	68	Use the following family counseling techniques: multigenerational
.00449	134	Supervise counselor trainees
.00448	62	Provide consultation services for professional skill development
.00435	52	Prepare developmental/preventative media

Combined index value	Item number	Work behavior
.00434	144	Develop program-related reports
.00433	140	Allocate financial resources for counseling program
.00428	54	Conduct self-development training for nonclients
.00424	57	Provide consultation services for organizational development
.00421	55	Provide multicultural training/education
.00407	105	Provide career counseling for older adults
.00380	142	Use computers for program data management
.00364	72	Counsel concerning premarriage
.00363	96	Provide outplacement counseling
.00356	124	Engage in data analyses
.00355	132	Write communication for noncounseling, professional activities
.00329	125	Collaborate in research with other professionals
.00296	18	Use computerized "counseling" software
.00289	119	Engage in counseling outcome research
.00289	118	Engage in counseling process research
.00282	131	Write for publication
.00278	102	Provide career counseling for children
.00270	126	Develop appraisal instrument/technique
.00249	120	Engage in field/observational research
.00219	127	Evaluate computer software
.00173	143	Conduct fund-raising activities for program development/maintenance
.00140	121	Engage in experimental/laboratory research

Chapter 6

DISCUSSION AND SUMMARY

A work behavior study (i.e., job analysis) can be effective only to the extent to which the items actually evaluated are meaningful for and pertinent to the respondents. The iterative, multiphase process used in this study was implemented successfully with this criterion in mind. Literally every person in the counseling profession had the opportunity to contribute work behaviors for consideration for inclusion, and literally hundreds of professional counselors had the opportunity to provide input about the forms of the items to be included in the survey. Numerous other professionals provided input about the final form of the survey distributed. Thus, the survey distributed was one that had both items and a format that readily could be interpreted by professional counselors.

Respondents in this study were all NCCs who effectively represented a cross section of those who identify themselves as professional counselors. More specifically, the sample encompassed appropriately proportionate numbers of counselors in regard to their varying professional credentials, personal characteristics, and employment settings. Because the respondents literally represented all major facets of the counseling profession, it is reasonable to assume that their responses also effectively represented the nature of work behaviors in the counseling profession.

The comprehensiveness and diversity of the sample has several important implications when considerating the results of this study. For example, the sample was of sufficient size so that the statistical analyses applied could be used with confidence; the basic theoretical assumptions underlying them were not violated. More important, however, the nature of the sample implies that the results were derived primarily from practicing professionals. The results reflect the realities of counseling practice, rather than esoteric opinions of what counseling practice is supposed to be.

Factor analysis was the primary data analytic technique used in this study, and the results of the factor analyses were clear and meaningful. Of particular significance is that the orthogonal and oblique solutions for both the FREQUENCY and IMPORTANCE data sets were essentially similar. Five relatively independent orthogonal factors were found in both data sets. This means that the resultant clusters of items were relatively distinct from one another in the minds of most of the respondents. Relatedly, although a relatively high factor loading criterion was used, the emergence of five highly similar factors (i.e., item clusters) in both the FREQUENCY and IMPORTANCE data sets attests to the distinctiveness of the item clusters. Thus, it can be inferred that the respondents made relatively clear distinctions among the various types of work behaviors and did so thoughtfully and carefully. The collective implication, then, based on results of the factor analyses, is that the respondents participated in the study conscientiously, thus enhancing the credibility of study results.

It might be inferred from cursory consideration of the data in Tables 14 and 15 that there are substantial differences in the work behaviors and professional perspectives among different counselors. However, further scrutiny of those data reveals some not-so-surprising results, and the differences therefore are not all that substantial. In particular, a vast majority of the significant differences identified in both the FREQUENCY and IMPORTANCE responses data are on the basis of employment setting and are in the Counseling for Career Development and the Professional Practices clusters. Traditionally, career development counseling has been emphasized as a focal point in the provision of counseling services for persons in middle and secondary schools and in colleges and universities. Therefore, it is not surprising that counselors in academic/educational settings engage in these related work behaviors more frequently, nor is it surprising that they view them as more important. Conversely, career development counseling has not been emphasized greatly by counselors in community settings (e.g., community mental health agencies or private practice), and, therefore, it would not be expected that the activities therein would be as *relatively* frequent among or of importance to counselors in community settings.

In a similar manner, professional practice activities (e.g., research, involvement in professional organizations, publishing, and consultation) have been emphasized to a greater extent for counselors in academic/educational settings than for those in community settings. Thus, the differences and the directions of the differences are not surprising for the Professional Practice items.

In general, it appears that the differences in the frequencies and importances of the various work behaviors are primarily a function of the "reward systems" extant in academic/educational and community settings. That is, rewards such as monetary increments and/or professional recognitions usually follow from effective fulfillment of expected activities. Moreover, professionals like to believe that the activities in which they engage are important ones. Therefore, it is easily understandable that counselors in different types of settings would differentially engage in work behaviors deemed appropriate to the respective settings and also differentially value or rate as important the activities in which they engage. Thus, although it might be inferred that there are at least two major "factions" within the counseling profession, it is far more reasonable to conclude that professional counselors readily adopt the (a) work-behavior expectations of their respective employment settings and (b) work-behavior importance perspectives appropriate to those settings.

Inherent in the item prioritization data is that counseling is what professional counselors do and value most. This is not a supercilious comment. Counseling practitioners' perspectives on what they do and why they do it are not always in accord with the "experts'" or even professional organizations' perspectives about what is important, and why, in the counseling profession. Again, clearly the respondents in this study represented the "mainstream" of the counseling profession, and, therefore, the results should be applicable to the vast majority of persons who identify themselves as professional counselors.

The major goal of this study, to develop a base of counselor work behaviors for the NCE, was accomplished. The resulting clusters of work behaviors are listed in Table 18. Included are essentially the same items presented in Table 16; however, a few work behaviors have been reworded slightly, and the order of item clusters has been rearranged.

Table 18
Prioritized Within Cluster Final Work Behavior List

Fundamental Counseling Practices

Counsel clients concerning personal change
Establish counseling goals
Assess potential for client to harm self/others
Evaluate client's movement toward counseling goals
Evaluate extent of client's psychological dysfunction
Counsel adults
Clarify counselor/client roles
Develop comprehensive treatment plans
Assist with client's evaluation of counseling
Reframe client's problem
Identify source-of-problem alternatives
Obtain client's informed consent prior to counseling
Counsel clients concerning life-style change
Inform client about ethical standards and practice
Clarify client's support systems
Assess psychosocial needs
Systematically observe client behaviors
Evaluate need for client referral
Evaluate existing (precounseling) client data
Conduct precounseling diagnostic interview
Use "active listening" skills
Maintain case notes, records, and/or files
Use cognitive-oriented counseling techniques
Self-evaluate counseling effectiveness
Inform client about legal aspects of counseling
Use behavioral-oriented counseling techniques
Determine DSM-III-R classification
Analyze cost-benefit of treatment alternatives

Counseling for Career Development

Assist client in understanding test results
Facilitate client's development of decision-making skills
Use test results for client decision making
Use interest inventories

Evaluate client's educational preparations
Use self-report personality inventories
Use test/inventory results for intervention selections
Evaluate client's occupational skills
Use occupational information in counseling
Provide career/vocational education
Facilitate client's development of job-search skills
Use achievement tests
Provide career counseling for adolescents
Use print and other media in career counseling
Select appraisal instruments/techniques for counseling
Provide career counseling for adults
Use nontest appraisal techniques
Use aptitude tests
Use career resources library
Use intelligence tests
Use computerized career counseling resources
Provide career counseling for persons with disabilities
Provide group vocational counseling
Provide career counseling for older adults
Provide outplacement counseling
Use computerized "counseling" software

Counseling Groups

Assist with group members' feedback to each other
Identify harmful group-member behaviors
Evaluate progress toward group goals
Resolve conflict among group members
Self-evaluate group counseling effectiveness
Determine group counseling termination criteria
Inform clients of group counseling guidelines and goals
Systematically observe group members' behaviors
Use "structured" activities during group counseling
Use group-centered group counseling leadership techniques
Use leader-centered group counseling leadership techniques

Counseling Families

Counsel persons in crisis
Counsel clients concerning substance use/abuse
Counsel clients concerning sexual abuse
Counsel adolescents
Counsel concerning family member interaction
Counsel clients concerning personality change
Counsel clients concerning physical abuse
Develop family conflict resolution strategies
Counsel concerning family change
Clarify family counseling goals
Clarify familial behavior norms
Inform family members of family dynamics/roles
Inform family members of family counseling guide lines and goals
Clarify client's moral/spiritual issues
Counsel concerning divorce
Counsel children
Counsel concerning human sexuality
Counsel concerning divorce-conflict reduction
Interview client's significant others
Use behavioral family counseling techniques
Counsel concerning marriage enrichment
Use structural family counseling techniques
Use strategic family counseling techniques
Use multigenerational family counseling techniques
Counsel concerning premarriage

Professional Practice

Serve as a liaison with other agencies
Provide consultation services for ethical or legal dilemmas
Participate in case conferences
Administer counseling program
Conduct prevention-oriented developmental activities
Participate in staffing decision-making processes
Engage in professional/community public relations
Participate in continuing education/skill enhancement
Conduct community outreach
Correspond orally with others to maintain professional communications
Evaluate counselors' performance
Establish programmatic service goals
Read current professional literature
Write to other professionals to maintain professional communications
Participate in professional organization activities
Assess programmatic needs
Review legal statutes and regulations
Supervise staff
Provide counselor skill-development training
Review ethical standards
Provide consultation services for interpersonal skills training
Provide consultation services for human relationships development
Provide consultation services for human resource needs evaluation
Engage in formative evaluation of counseling program
Engage in summative evaluation of counseling program
Supervise counselor trainees
Provide consultation services for professional skill development
Prepare developmental/preventative media
Develop program-related reports
Allocate financial resources for counseling program
Conduct self-development training for nonclients
Provide consultation services for organizational development
Provide multicultural training/education

Use computers for program data management
Engage in data analyses
Write communication for noncounseling, professional activities
Collaborate in research with other professionals
Engage in counseling outcome research
Engage in counseling process research

Write for publication
Provide career counseling for children
Develop appraisal instrument/technique
Engage in field/observational research
Evaluate computer software
Conduct fund-raising activities for program development/maintenance
Engage in experimental/laboratory research

REFERENCES

American Educational Research Association, American Psychological Association, and National Council on Measurement in Education. (1985). *Standards for educational and psychological testing*. Washington, DC: American Psychological Association.

Amick, D. J., & Walberg, H. J. (Eds.). (1975). *Introductory multivariate analysis for educational, psychological, and social research*. Berkeley, CA: McCutchan.

Belkin, G. S. (1988). *Introduction to counseling* (3rd ed.). Dubuque, IA: Brown.

Borg, W. R., & Gall, M. D. (1989). *Educational research: An introduction* (5th ed.). New York: Longman.

Brown, D., & Srebalus, D. J. (1988). *An introduction to the counseling profession*. Englewood Cliffs, NJ: Prentice-Hall.

California revamps examinations process. *CLEAR News*, (1990, Winter), pp. 1, 3, 5.

Capuzzi, D., & Gross, D. R. (Eds.). (1991). *Introduction to counseling*. Boston: Allyn & Bacon.

Crocker, L. & Algina, J. (1986). *Introduction to classical and modern test theory*. New York: Holt, Rinehart & Winston.

Dameron, J. (Ed.). (1980). *The professional counselor: Competencies, performance guidelines, and assessment*. Alexandria, VA: American Personnel and Guidance Association.

Educational Testing Service. (1982). *Inventory of responsibilities of licensed psychologists*. Princeton, NJ: Center for Occupational and Professional Assessment, Educational Testing Service.

Eichelberger, R. T. (1989). *Disciplined inquiry: Understanding and doing educational research*. New York: Longman.

Fine, S. A. (1986). Job analysis. In R. A. Berk (Ed.), *Performance assessment: Methods & applications* (pp. 53-81). Baltimore, MD: Johns Hopkins University Press.

Fitzgerald, L. F., & Osipow, S. H. (1986). An occupational analysis of counseling psychology. *Journal of Counseling Psychology, 41*, 535-544.

Gibson, R. L., & Mitchell, M. H. (1986). *Introduction to counseling and guidance* (2nd ed.). New York: Macmillan.

Gladding, S. T. (1988). *Counseling: A comprehensive profession*. Columbus, OH: Merrill.

Glasnapp, D. R., & Poggio, J. P. (1985). *Essentials of statistical analysis for the behavioral sciences*. Columbus, OH: Merrill.

Harman, H. (1976). *Modern factor analysis*. Chicago: University of Chicago Press.

Harvey, R. J. (1986). Quantative approaches to job classification: A review and critique. *Personnel Psychology, 39*, 267-289.

Harvey, R. J., & Lozada-Larsen, S. R. (1988). Influence of amount of job descriptive information on job analysis rating accuracy. *Journal of Applied Psychology, 73*, 457-461.

Hays, W. L. (1988). *Statistics* (4th ed.). New York: Holt, Rinehart and Winston.

Howell, D. C. (1989). *Fundamental statistics for the behavioral sciences* (2nd ed.). Boston: PWS Kent.

Kachigan, S. K. (1986). *Statistical analysis An interdisciplinary introduction to univariate & multivariate methods*. New York: Radius Press.

Kane, M. T., Kingsbury, C., Colton, D., & Estes, C. (1989). Combining data on criticality and frequency in developing test plans for licensure and certification examinations. *Journal of Educational Measurement, 26*, 17-27.

Kerlinger, F. N. (1986). *Foundations of behavioral research*. New York: Holt, Rinehart and Winston.

Kraemer, H. C., & Thiemann, S. (1987). *How many subjects? Statistical power analysis in research*. Newbury Park, CA: Sage.

Lewis, M. D., Hayes, R. L., & Lewis, J. A. (Eds.). (1992). *An introduction to the counseling profession* (2nd ed.). Istasca, IL: Peacock.

Linn, R. L. (1985). Developments and trends in licensing and licensing examinations (pp. 185-198). In J. C. Fortune & Associates, *Understanding testing in occupational licensing*. Washington, DC: Jossey-Bass.

Lipsey, M. W. (1990). *Design sensitivity*. Newbury Park, CA: Sage.

Loesch, L. C. & Vacc, N. A. (1991). *National counselor examination technical manual* (1991 rev.). Greensboro, NC: National Board for Certified Counselors.

Mulaik, S. A. (1972). *The foundations of factor analysis*. New York: McGraw-Hill.

National Association of Alcoholism and Drug Abuse Counselors. (1986). *Development of model profession standards for counselor credentialing*. Arlington, VA: National Association of Alcoholism and Drug Abuse Counselors Education and Research Institute.

Nugent, F. A. (1990). *An introduction to the counseling profession*. Columbus, OH: Merrill.

Peterson, J. V., & Nisenholz, B. (1987). *Orientation to counseling*. Boston: Allyn & Bacon.

Raymond, M. (1990, Winter). Abstract and updates: Job analysis. *CLEAR Exam Review*. pp. 9-11.

Sanchez, J. I., & Levine, E. L. (1989). Determining important tasks within jobs: A policy-capturing approach. *Journal of Applied Psychology*, *74*, 336-342.

Schafer, W. D. (1990). Interpreting statistical significance. *Measurement and Evaluation in Counseling and Development*, *23*, 98-99.

Shimberg, B., & Rosenfeld, M. (1990, Winter). Psychometric issues job analysis: Key to content valid tests. *CLEAR Exam Review*, pp. 14-15.

Smith, I. L., & Hambleton, R. K. (1990, Winter). Content validity studies of licensing examinations. *Educational Measurement: Issues and Practices*, 7-10.

State of Florida. (1987). *Mental health counselor occupational survey report*. Tallahassee, FL: Office Examination Services, Department of Professional Regulation.

Thompson, B. (1989). Statistical significance, result importance, and result generalizability: Three noteworthy but somewhat different issues. *Measurement and Evaluation in Counseling and Development*, *22*), 25.

Vacc, N.A., & Loesch, L.C. (1993). *Counseling as a profession* (2nd ed.). Muncie, IN: Accelerated Development.

APPENDIX A

Work Behavior Solicitation Announcement

NBCC Seeks Counselor Work Behavior Statements

The National Board for Certified Counselors (NBCC) is coordinating a large scale project that focuses on the development of a comprehensive description of the work of professionals who identify themselves as **practicing professional counselors.** This description eventually will include both professional counselors' work behaviors and the competencies necessary to perform those work behaviors effectively. The first step in this process is the compilation of a set of work behaviors in which professional counselors typically engage. Your assistance is being sought to identify those work behaviors.

A **work behavior statement** is a description of a specific behavior performed by counselors as a part of regular professional activity; i.e., **a description of what counselors actually do in their daily work.** You can create work behavior statements by monitoring and taking note of the activities in which you engage in your work as a professional counselor.

Work behavior statements are needed for both direct service and other activities performed by professional counselors. Direct service activities include functions such as individual and group counseling, assessment/appraisal, career/-lifestyle counseling, research, and consultation. Other professional activities include functions such as supervision, professional development, case management, professional organization involvements, public relations, and service/program evaluation.

Specificity in work behavior statements (i.e., nature, purpose, clientele, and setting) is highly desirable. Examples of work behavior statements for direct service activities include "individual counseling with a child to improve the child's relationships with peers" and "assessing the vocational interests of a midlife adult male." Examples of work behavior statements for other professional activities include "making case notes" and "attending a workshop to improve vocational counseling skills."

Your assistance with this important professional project will be greatly appreciated. Please take the time to monitor your (typical) work activities for a week or so and to describe those activities as work behavior statements. Please send your work behavior statements to: Dr. Larry Loesch, University of Florida, 1215 Norman Hall, Gainesville, FL 32611.

APPENDIX B

Letter of Request and Instructions to Reviewers of Initial Work Behavior Statement List

May 23, 1990

Dear Professional Colleague,

From previous correspondence and/or articles in various professional newsletters, you are aware that NBCC is conducting a multiphase project intended to lead eventually to competency-based forms of the National Counselor Examination (NCE). The first phase, in which widespread solicitation was used to obtain "work behavior statements" from professionals who identify themselves as counselors, is now complete. The edited result of that effort, approximately 330 work behavior statements, is attached for your review and use.

In the third phase of this process the (remaining) work behavior statements will be distributed to a large and diverse group of professional counselors who will be asked to provide data about the frequencies with which they engage in the work behaviors listed and the relative importances of the those behaviors in their professional counseling activities. The resultant data will be analyzed to identify generic counselor work behaviors, i.e., those engaged in most frequently and judged to be most important to the work of all counselors. Subsequently, competencies related to the counselors' generic work behaviors will be created and the NCE items related to those competencies.

Prior to initiation of the third phase, it is necessary and desirable to reduce the number of work behaviors to be evaluated. Therefore, we are seeking your assistance with the second phase of this project. You have been selected to be involved in this phase in recognition of your many professional accomplishments, involvements, and understandings. Please know that only about fifty professionals are being invited to participate in this phase, and therefore that your assistance is important, highly valued, and appreciated.

The task at hand is to reduce the list of work behavior statements as much as possible, but without limiting the potential applicabilities of the remaining items.

We believe that the list can be reduced by approximately one-third (to a range of 200 to 250 statements), but no restrictions are placed on how you modify the list. The goal of this phase is to develop a list of work behavior statements that are potentially applicable to all professionals who identify themselves as counselors. Your assistance in modifying, editing, or otherwise condensing the statements on the attached list with that goal in mind would be appreciated tremendously. The list has been presented doublespaced to facilitate modification; please feel free to mark on it.

When you have completed making modifications on the list, please return it in the envelope provided. In order for the project to proceed as scheduled, it will be neccessary to receive your list by July 16; earlier if possible.

We realize that your time is valuable and we are sorry that we cannot pay you for your assistance. However, please know that the results of a couple of hours of your work will be extremely helpful and significant in this important professional endeavor.

Thank you for your assistance.

Sincerely,

Larry C. Loesch, Ph.D., NCC
NBCC Evaluations Coordinator

Nicholas A. Vacc, Ed.D., NCC
NBCC Examination Consultant

APPENDIX C

Initial Work Behavior Statement List and Retention/Deletion Recommendations

Work behavior statement	Retain-delete
Administer precounseling intake/interview form	24-4
Plan counseling program activities	20-8
Solicit and select employees (i.e., counselors)	16-12
Provide feedback on counseling effectiveness to staff counselors	18-10
Determine and administrate task assignments and responsibilities	14-14
Solicit/seek counseling program resources	19-9
Conduct formal counselor staff evaluations	16-12
Conduct programmatic needs assessment	18-10
Represent counseling agency at governmental/administrative meetings	12-16
Fulfill "public relations" functions on behalf of counseling staff and/or agency	21-7
Fulfill interagency liaison role and functions	16-12
Develop counseling program budget and/or allocations	18-10
Prepare counseling program summary reports	20-8
Coordinate (counseling) staff development activities	15-13
Develop counseling program admission/eligibility criteria and procedures	16-12
Review legal statutes pertinent to counseling program/staff activities	20-8
Develop community outreach programs	17-11
Coordinate (counseling) fund-raising activities	9-19
Coordinate interagency referral processes	20-8
Develop funding proposals	14-14
Evaluate computer software potentially useful for clients and/or counseling program	23-5
Coordinate peer counseling programs	16-12
Recruit and select peer counselors	14-14

Work behavior statement	Retain-delete
Conduct (counseling) program orientation activities for potential clients	20-8
Coordinate (lead) case conferences	26-2
Coordinate community placement programs for clients	7-21
Interpret and administer state/local governmental regulations pertinent to counseling program	18-10
Evaluate periodic (e.g., daily or monthly) reports submitted by counseling staff	16-12
Facilitate intraprogram communications and relationships among counseling staff	18-10
Administer aptitude tests	21-7
Administer achievement tests	21-7
Administer individual intelligence tests	17-11
Administer group intelligence tests	21-7
Administer career/vocational interest inventories	21-7
Administer self-report (i.e., paper-and-pencil) personality inventories	19-9
Administer projective personality inventories	4-24
Evaluate appraisal instrument/technique technical data	19-9
Interpret standardized test data	24-4
Interpret nonstandardized test data	24-4
Select appraisal instruments/techniques for use in counseling	24-4
Apply sociometric appraisal/assessment techniques	9-19
Administer neuropsychological tests	5-23
Administer perceptual-motor tests	6-22
Interpret psychophysiological measures (e.g., GSR or EEG)	5-23
Develop (test performance) expectancy tables	4-24
Administer measures of values	4-24
Administer measures of attitudes	8-20
Administer questionnaires and/or surveys	17-11
Help clients develop job search skills	2-26

Work behavior statement	Retain-delete
Help clients develop (job search) resumes	15-13
Conduct individual career/vocational counseling	24-4
Develop career education programming	20-8
Help clients find occupational information	20-8
Help clients use career/vocational computerized resources	25-3
Help clients develop decision-making skills	23-5
Interpret test results for/with clients	20-8
Help clients develop test-taking skills	18-10
Conduct/coordinate "mock interviews" for clients seeking jobs	14-14
Help job-seeking clients evaluate their educational backgrounds	21-7
Help job-seeking clients evaluate their vocational skills	18-10
Refer clients for vocational rehabilitation services and/or counseling	23-5
Help clients do job task analyses	7-21
Analyze/evaluate local area employment situations	20-8
Coordinate (post)career counseling placement activities	20-8
Assess vocational potentials of clients with disabilities	20-8
Write up case notes	23-5
Maintain case records and/or files	23-5
Perform client billing activities	10-18
Review client file data prior to counseling sessions	21-7
Conduct behavioral observations prior to counseling	19-9
Develop comprehensive treatment plans	26-2
Supervise clients' community placement activities	19-9
Prepare discharge reports and plans	15-13
Conduct follow-up contacts with former clients	18-10

Work behavior statement	Retain-delete
Conduct diagnostic clinical interviews	22-6
Evaluate clients' previous counseling histories	21-7
Use computers for client data management	15-13
Negotiate fees with clients	8-20
Identify placement needs for special population clients	2-17
Identify institutional/agency placement resources	15-13
Identify interagency counseling resources	15-13
Provide counseling approach/technique assistance to other counselors	22-6
Conduct counseling needs assessments	22-6
Write consultation reports	22-6
Provide expert witness testimony	15-13
Evaluate program operation effectiveness	19-9
Consult with parents of child counselees	25-3
Help to identify clients with special needs	23-5
Facilitate school/community agency counseling program relationships	16-12
Provide organizational development services	15-13
Serve as a member of a child study/evaluation team	15-13
Facilitate identification of organizational problems	15-13
Evaluate the human resources needs of an organization	16-12
Provide classroom management techniques training/assistance	17-11
Help colleagues to understand research results	20-8
Facilitate development of intraorganization human relationships resources	10-18
Consult with physicians regarding clients' physical/health conditions	20-8
Consult with attorneys regarding clients' legal rights and situations	20-8
Obtain client information from other counseling agencies	20-8

Work behavior statement	Retain-delete
Provide large group guidance activities	5-23
Provide self-development (e.g., assertiveness) training	25-3
Conduct drug education/awareness activities	23-5
Conduct conflict resolution skills training	25-3
Provide developmental guidance activities for members of the local community	10-18
Conduct self-esteem/self-concept enhancement activities	24-4
Interpret/explain stages of human growth and development to clients	25-3
Maintain a "personal development" library for clients	11-17
Conduct sex education activities	17-11
Conduct multi- and/or cross-cultural relationships facilitation activities	26-2
Conduct physical abuse prevention activities	23-5
Conduct sexual abuse prevention activities	23-5
Provide divorce adjustment activities for children or adults	18-10
Facilitate sex-role development discussions	21-7
Provide premarriage counseling	10-18
Conduct time management seminars and presentations	5-23
Provide services for adult children of alcoholics	21-7
Collect precounseling information from potential group members	24-4
Evaluate clients for participation in counseling groups	27-1
Establish group counseling schedules	11-17
Clarify group counseling goals	18-10
Describe group counseling "ground rules" and guidelines	20-8
Systematically observe counseling group members' interactive behaviors	17-11

Work behavior statement	Retain-delete
Solicit counseling group members' feedback and evaluations on counseling effectiveness	17-11
Solicit counseling group members' feedback on leader behaviors and performance	18-10
Lead personal adjustment/growth group counseling	17-11
Lead task group counseling	14-14
Lead self-exploration group counseling	13-15
Lead drug use/abuse group counseling	12-16
Lead human sexuality group counseling	11-17
Lead group counseling for sexually abused persons	12-16
Lead group counseling for physically abused persons	12-16
Lead social skills training groups	12-16
Lead group counseling for children of divorce	12-16
Lead divorce/separation group counseling	12-16
Lead group counseling for persons with conduct disorders	11-17
Lead group counseling for grieving persons	13-15
Lead group counseling for adult children of alcoholics	12-16
Provide test interpretations in a group context	16-12
Make self-disclosure statements during group counseling	13-15
Use prepackaged/structured activities within group counseling	11-17
Resolve conflicts between counseling group members	11-17
Provide individual assistance to a counseling group member outside of the group context	15-13
Intervene when group members' behaviors are harmful to specific individuals	17-11
Evaluate a counseling group's progress towards its goals	2-26
Decide when group counseling should be discontinued	20-8
Use psychoanalytic group counseling techniques	5-23
Use behavioral group counseling techniques	8-20
Use person-centered group counseling techniques	8-20
Use Gestalt group counseling techniques	8-20

Work behavior statement	Retain-delete
Use transactional analysis group counseling techniques	6-22
Use humanistic group counseling techniques	10-18
Use existential group counseling techniques	6-22
Use systemic group counseling techniques	8-20
Use rational-emotive group counseling techniques	7-21
Use reality therapy group counseling techniques	7-21
Use multimodal group counseling techniques	8-20
Use stress management techniques in group counseling	8-20
Observe/note client behaviors during individual counseling	8-20
Observe/note client behaviors outside the context of counseling	12-16
Help clients clarify their problems	23-5
Establish counseling goals for clients	20-8
Help clients establish counseling goals	24-4
Do (psycho)diagnostic work in individual counseling	16-12
Establish a probable schedule for each individual counseling client	20-8
Solicit individual counseling clients' perceptions of counseling outcomes	22-6
Subjectively evaluate individual counseling outcomes	24-4
Formally/systematically evaluate individual counseling outcomes	23-5
Provide short-term (brief) individual counseling	26-2
Help clients clarify their support systems	25-3
Help clients identify additional counseling resources	24-4
Conduct long-term (i.e., more than 8 weeks) individual counseling	23-5
Provide individual human sexuality counseling	11-17
Provide individual drug use/abuse counseling	12-15

Work behavior statement	Retain-delete
Provide individual counseling for relief of depression	13-15
Refer clients to other counseling practitioners or agencies	15-13
Provide individual alcohol use/abuse counseling	10-18
Provide individual divorce/separation counseling	11-17
Provide individual behavioral adjustment/improvement counseling	12-16
Provide individual suicide prevention counseling	12-16
Provide individual birth control counseling	11-17
Provide individual abortion decision counseling	10-18
Provide individual grief/death-and-dying counseling	10-18
Provide individual environmental displacement counseling	10-18
Provide individual counseling for status offenders	11-17
Provide individual counseling for physically abused persons	11-17
Provide individual counseling for sexually abused persons	11-17
Provide individual counseling for crime victims	12-16
Provide individual counseling for persons with physical disabilities	11-17
Provide individual counseling for persons with emotional disabilities	11-17
Provide individual counseling for persons with sexual identity problems	12-16
Provide individual counseling to help persons cope with relatives experiencing mental health problems	13-15
Provide individual counseling for adult children of alcoholics	11-17
Provide biofeedback training for stress reduction	12-16
Arrange furniture to accommodate clients' physical characteristics	15-13
Provide individual bibliotherapy counseling	16-12
Help clients clarify moral and/or spiritual issues	21-7

Work behavior statement	Retain-delete
Provide individual counseling for abused older persons	16-13
Determine a client's DSM-III-R classification	21-7
Provide individual leisure counseling	6-22
Provide individual preretirement counseling	9-19
Refer a client to a medical services provider	19-9
Provide individual counseling for adaptation by formerly incarcerated persons	9-19
Collect "personal history" information from a client	18-10
Conduct a cost-benefit analysis of treatment alternatives	11-17
Obtain clients' informed consents for counseling treatments to be used	22-6
Conduct a psychosocial needs assessment for/of a client	23-5
Use humor in individual counseling processes	20-8
Explain/clarify the nature of counseling for individual clients	24-4
Explain the concept of confidentiality to individual clients	24-4
Use role-playing techniques in individual counseling processes	24-4
Help clients understand alternative hypotheses that clarify the client's situation	20-8
Provide play counseling for children	14-14
"Reframe" a client's problem to facilitate the client's understanding	26-2
Provide individual systematic desensitization counseling	11-17
Provide individual dream interpretation counseling	22-6
Provide interpretations of appraisal data in individual counseling	21-7
Use art therapy techniques in individual counseling	6-22
Use art/media techniques for diagnostic purposes in individual counseling	9-19

Work behavior statement	Retain-delete
Clarify counselor and client roles in individual counseling	2-26
Interview significant others in a client's life to facilitate understanding of the client	19-9
Assess a client's potential for harm to self	27-1
Assess a client's potential for harm to others	25-3
Self evaluate individual counseling abilities	22-6
Evaluate formally a client's progress during individual counseling	21-7
Evaluate a client's motivation for counseling	22-6
Determine termination criteria for individual counseling	22-6
Use psychoanalytic techniques in individual counseling	5-23
Use behavioral techniques in individual counseling	10-18
Use person-centered techniques in individual counseling	11-17
Use Gestalt techniques in individual counseling	9-19
Use transactional analysis techniques in individual counseling	8-20
Use existential techniques in individual counseling	7-21
Use humanistic techniques in individual counseling	10-18
Use systemic techniques in individual counseling	8-20
Use rational-emotive techniques in individual counseling	10-18
Use reality therapy techniques in individual counseling	10-18
Use multimodal techniques in individual counseling	9-19
Use hypnosis techniques in individual counseling	4-24
Use biofeedback techniques in individual counseling	6-22
Use active listening techniques in individual counseling	2-53
Construct family genograms	5-23
Explain family dynamics concepts to clients	14-14
Conduct family counseling using systemic techniques	12-16

Work behavior statement	Retain-delete
Conduct home environment visitations/evaluations	7-21
Help family members develop conflict resolution strategies	18-10
Help family members understand familial norms of behavior	15-13
Diagnose a family's level of functionality	10-18
Determine the identified patient in a family	12-16
Evaluate the developmental levels of respective members of a family	10-18
Formulate a family counseling treatment plan	10-8
Select appropriate appraisal instruments/techniques for use in family counseling	5-23
Conduct conjoint family counseling	6-22
Use art therapy techniques in the context of family counseling	3-25
Establish counseling program service goals	23-5
Conduct formative counseling program evaluations	11-17
Conduct summative counseling program evaluations	11-17
Develop counseling program evaluation materials	12-16
Evaluate outcomes of clients' community placements	3-25
Attend state-level professional association/organization meetings	18-10
Attend national-level professional association/organization meetings	19-9
Present skill development workshops at professional association/organization conferences	18-10
Engage in professional continuing education/development activities	25-3
Present research results at professional meetings	15-13
Serve on professional association/organization committees and/or task forces	18-10
Serve as an elected official of a professional association/organization	9-19
Contribute materials for professional newsletters	13-15
Serve on an editorial board for a professional publication	6-22

Work behavior statement	Retain-delete
Serve as an editor of a professional publication	3-25
Serve as a member of a professional credentialing board	6-22
Assist with counselor education program accreditation activities	7-21
Develop print media for use in developmental counseling activities	8-20
Develop print media to describe counseling services offered	12-16
Serve as a client advocate in a legal system (e.g., court)	12-16
Develop accountability procedures and guidelines	12-16
Obtain pertinent professional credentials	14-14
Write letters of recommendation	11-17
Develop activities to countermand societal prejudices	9-19
Coordinate activities to enhance intergenerational relationships	7-21
Coordinate activities to enhance intercultural relationships	8-20
Facilitate counselor education program development	6-22
Review professional ethical standards	23-5
Conduct systematic reviews of professional literature	17-11
Formulate research questions	5-23
Formulate research hypotheses	7-21
Evaluate research designs	6-22
Conduct data analyses	6-22
Conduct research-related assessments	6-22
Conduct counseling process research	19-9
Develop appraisal instruments/techniques for use in counseling	8-20
Conduct field-based (observational) counseling research	13-15
Conduct research in counseling laboratory settings	6-22
Develop grant proposals	6-22
Collaborate in research with other professionals	9-19

Work behavior statement	Retain-delete
Conduct counseling outcome research	9-19
Analyze existing data bases (e.g., through meta-analyses)	3-25
Identify areas of counseling for which research is needed	6-22
Monitor adherence to ethical standards for research	6-22
Conduct local area demography surveys of potential clients	3-25
Develop questionnaires and opinionnaires	5-23
Develop rating scales	6-22
Provide individual supervision for aspiring counselors	9-19
Conduct group supervision for aspiring counselors	9-19
Write supervision reports	10-18
Analyze counselors' skills levels	8-20
Review and critique audiotapes	6-22
Review and critique videotapes	6-22
Provide demonstrations of counseling techniques	12-16
Help other professionals resolve ethical dilemmas	10-18
Conduct role-playing/role-reversal activities for supervisees	6-22
Clarify a counseling approach for another professional	8-20
Provide media resources for supervisees	4-24
Assist supervisees in case report development	6-22
Assist supervisees with test data interpretations	6-22
Provide formal feedback to supervisees on counseling effectiveness	11-17
Provide counselor trainee practicum/internship on-site supervision	10-18
Make public presentations on achieving mental health	9-19
Teach courses to aspiring counselors	22-6
Evaluate counselor trainees' academic performance	22-6
Contribute to development of counselor education course materials	4-24

Work behavior statement	Retain-delete
Serve as an advisor to a student group	5-23
Contribute to development of counselor education curricula	3-25
Provide inservice training for noncounseling professionals	7-21
Teach ethical decision-making strategies to noncounseling professionals	5-23
Write articles for professional journals	11-17
Serve as a reviewer for grant applications	4-24
Write for "lay" publications (e.g., newspapers or magazines)	4-24
Write (all or part of) professional books	2-26

APPENDIX D

Counselors' Work Behavior Study

Survey Instrument

[actual survey presented on the pages following]

NATIONAL BOARD FOR CERTIFIED COUNSELORS, INC.

March 18, 1991

Dear National Certified Counselor,

The National Board for Certified Counselors is conducting a survey of great significance to the counseling profession, in general, and to all who identify themselves as professional counselors in particular. The purpose of this survey is to develop a profile of the work behaviors of professional counselors. Because such a survey has never before been undertaken on a national basis for professionals who identify themselves as counselors, the results will be critically important for our profession. One specific outcome of this project will be reformulation of the NBCC's National Counselor Examination to reflect more accurately the roles and functions of professional counselors. Other important outcomes will be related to aspects of counselor credentialing in general.

You have been selected as a respondent because of your status as a National Certified Counselor (NCC). Only a relatively small number of NCCs are being requested to respond because of the large cost involved in conducting this project. Therefore, your participation is highly desired and will be greatly appreciated! We realize fully that there are many important demands upon your time, but we sincerely hope that you will take the time to assist this project by completing the enclosed survey and returning it in the envelope provided. We cannot emphasize enough the importance to our profession of your participation in the study. We need your help.

Please return your completed response sheets in the envelope provided by April 19, 1991. On behalf of the National Board for Certified Counselors and all professional counselors, thank you for your assistance with this important project.

Sincerely,

Larry C. Loesch /ses

Larry C. Loesch, Ph.D., NCC

Nicholas A. Vacc

Nicholas A. Vacc, Ed.D., NCC

Thomas W. Clawson, Ed.D., NCC
NBCC Executive Director
5999 Stevenson Avenue
Alexandria, VA 22304
(703) 461-6222
(703) 823-1146, FAX

Larry C. Loesch, Ph.D., NCC
NBCC Research/Evaluation Consultant
University of Florida
Counselor Education Department
1215 Norman Hall
Gainesville, FL 32611
(904) 392-0731

James Sampson, Ph.D., NCC, NCCC
NBCC Career Evaluation Consultant
Florida State University
Department of Human Services & Studies
215 Stone Building
Tallahassee, FL 32306
(904) 644-3854/644-6431

Nicholas A. Vacc, Ed.D., NCC, CCMHC
NBCC Evaluation Consultant
University of North Carolina
Department of Counselor Education
220 Curry Building
Greensboro, NC 27412
(919) 334-5100

NBCC Work Behavior Study
INSTRUCTIONS

Please use only a #2 lead pencil for your responses and completely fill each circle. Responses are to be provided anonymously and therefore your name should not be included on any of the response sheets.

Step 1 -- providing needed information at the top of pages 1 and 3:

a. At the top of page 1 are three black squares followed by a series of circled numbers. Please fill in the number which corresponds with the highest degree program you have completed, as listed below:

1 Master's degree in counseling
2 Master's degree in a closely related area
3 Education Specialist degree in counseling
4 Education Specialist degree in a closely related area
5 Doctoral degree in counselor education
6 Doctoral degree in counseling psychology
7 Doctoral degree in other closely related field

b. At the top of page 3 are three black squares followed by a series of circled numbers. Please fill in the number that represents your primary professional work setting(s) as outlined below:

1 Academic (CACREP approved program)
2 Academic (non-CACREP approved program)
3 School
4 Post-secondary institution
5 Counseling center
6 Hospital
7 Research facility
8 Government agency
9 Private industry
10 Community mental health center
11 Private practice
12 Full-time counselor

Step 2 -- responding to the survey questions on pages 1 through 4

For each of 152 work behaviors listed on pages 1 through 4, you are to indicate the relative FREQUENCY with which you perform each in your professional capacity. Beginning with page 1 and using the rating scale outlined below, fill the circle of the number that best represents the degree to which you perform each work behavior:

1--Never 2--Rarely 3--Occasionally 4--Frequently 5--Routinely

Step 3 -- responding to the survey questions on pages 5 through 8:

For the 152 work behaviors listed on pages 5 through 8, you are to indicate the degree to which your counselees believe you should be able to perform each effectively. Beginning with page 5 and using the rating scale below, please fill in the circle of the number which best represents the degree of IMPORTANCE that your counselees would place on your being able to perform that behavior effectively. Additionally, at the end of the questionnaire there are three informational items; please respond as indicated.

1 Of no importance
2 Of little importance
3 Moderately important
4 Very important
5 Critically important

Step 4 -- returning the survey:

Please return only the response sheets in the envelope provided, by April 19, 1991. Thank you.

DO NOT WRITE IN THIS AREA

Use #2 pencil

FREQUENCY

WORK BEHAVIOR STUDY
RESPONSE FORM I

ROUTINELY 5
FREQUENTLY 4
OCCASIONALLY 3
RARELY 2
NEVER 1

		1	2	3	4	5
1.	Obtain client's informed consent prior to counseling	1	2	3	4	5
2.	**Evaluate existing (pre-counseling) client data**	1	2	3	4	5
3.	Develop comprehensive treatment plans	1	2	3	4	5
4.	**Assess psychosocial needs**	1	2	3	4	5
5.	Assess potential for client to harm self/others	1	2	3	4	5
6.	**Clarify client's support systems**	1	2	3	4	5
7.	Systematically observe client behaviors	1	2	3	4	5
8.	**Assist with client's evaluation of counseling**	1	2	3	4	5
9.	Self-evaluate counseling effectiveness	1	2	3	4	5
10.	**Maintain case notes, records, and/or files**	1	2	3	4	5
11.	Conduct former client follow-up activities	1	2	3	4	5
12.	**Conduct pre-counseling diagnostic interview**	1	2	3	4	5
13.	Establish counseling goals	1	2	3	4	5
14.	**Analyze cost-benefit of treatment alternatives**	1	2	3	4	5
15.	Determine DSMIII-R classification	1	2	3	4	5
16.	**Evaluate extent of client's psychological dysfunction**	1	2	3	4	5
17.	Reframe client's problem	1	2	3	4	5
18.	**Use computerized "counseling" software**	1	2	3	4	5
19.	Counsel short-term (less than 6 sessions)	1	2	3	4	5
20.	**Counsel long-term (6 sessions or longer)**	1	2	3	4	5
21.	Interview client's significant others	1	2	3	4	5
22.	**Research use of a specific counseling intervention**	1	2	3	4	5
23.	Counsel children	1	2	3	4	5
24.	**Counsel adolescents**	1	2	3	4	5
25.	Counsel adults	1	2	3	4	5
26.	**Counsel older persons**	1	2	3	4	5
27.	Counsel persons in crisis	1	2	3	4	5
28.	**Counsel clients concerning substance use/abuse**	1	2	3	4	5
39.	Counsel clients concerning personal change	1	2	3	4	5
30.	**Counsel clients concerning physical abuse**	1	2	3	4	5
31.	Counsel clients concerning lifestyle change	1	2	3	4	5
32.	**Counsel clients concerning personality change**	1	2	3	4	5
33.	Counsel clients concerning sexual abuse	1	2	3	4	5
34.	**Use "active listening" skills**	1	2	3	4	5
35.	Use affective-oriented counseling techniques	1	2	3	4	5
36.	**Use behavioral-oriented counseling techniques**	1	2	3	4	5
37.	Use cognitive-oriented counseling techniques	1	2	3	4	5
38.	**Use brief psychotherapy techniques**	1	2	3	4	5
39.	Use media resources in counseling	1	2	3	4	5
40.	**Inform client about human growth and development**	1	2	3	4	5

QUESTIONS CONTINUE ON BACK

Use #2 pencil

RESPONSE FORM I

FREQUENCY

ROUTINELY 5
FREQUENTLY 4
OCCASIONALLY 3
RARELY 2
NEVER 1

Item	1	2	3	4	5
41. Inform client about ethical standards and practice	1	2	3	4	5
42. Inform client about legal aspects of counseling	1	2	3	4	5
43. Evaluate need for client referral	1	2	3	4	5
44. Evaluate client's movement toward counseling goals	1	2	3	4	5
45. Clarify counselor/client role	1	2	3	4	5
46. Clarify client's moral/spiritual issues	1	2	3	4	5
47. Identify source-of-problem alternatives	1	2	3	4	5
48. Identify client's non-counseling resources	1	2	3	4	5
49. Provide human development education	1	2	3	4	5
50. Provide career/vocational education	1	2	3	4	5
51. Provide mental health enhancement training/education	1	2	3	4	5
52. Prepare developmental/preventative media	1	2	3	4	5
53. Conduct prevention-oriented developmental activities	1	2	3	4	5
54. Conduct self-development training for non-clients	1	2	3	4	5
55. Provide multicultural training/education	1	2	3	4	5
56. Participate in case conferences	1	2	3	4	5
57. Provide consultation services for organizational development	1	2	3	4	5
58. Provide consultation services for human relationships development	1	2	3	4	5
69. Provide consultation services for interpersonal skills training	1	2	3	4	5
60. Provide consultation services for human resource needs evaluation	1	2	3	4	5
61. Provide consultation services for ethical or legal dilemmas	1	2	3	4	5
62. Provide consultation services for professional skill development	1	2	3	4	5
63. Inform family members of family counseling guidelines and goals	1	2	3	4	5
64. Inform family of family dynamics/roles	1	2	3	4	5
65. Clarify familial behavior norms	1	2	3	4	5
66. Clarify family counseling goals	1	2	3	4	5
67. Develop family conflict resolution strategies	1	2	3	4	5
68. Use the following family counseling techniques: Multi-generational	1	2	3	4	5
79. Use the following family counseling techniques: Structural	1	2	3	4	5
70. Use the following family counseling techniques: Strategic	1	2	3	4	5
71. Use the following family counseling techniques: Behavioral	1	2	3	4	5
72. Counsel concerning pre-marriage	1	2	3	4	5
73. Counsel concerning divorce	1	2	3	4	5
74. Counsel concerning divorce-conflict reduction	1	2	3	4	5
75. Counsel concerning human sexuality	1	2	3	4	5
76. Counsel concerning marriage enrichment	1	2	3	4	5
77. Counsel concerning family change	1	2	3	4	5
78. Counsel concerning family member interaction	1	2	3	4	5
79. Inform clients of group counseling guidelines and goals	1	2	3	4	5
80. Systematically observe group members' behaviors	1	2	3	4	5

DO NOT WRITE IN THIS AREA

Use #2 pencil

RESPONSE FORM I

FREQUENCY

NEVER 1 · RARELY 2 · OCCASIONALLY 3 · FREQUENTLY 4 · ROUTINELY 5

Item	1	2	3	4	5
81. Identify harmful group-member behaviors	1	2	3	4	5
82. Evaluate progress toward group goals	1	2	3	4	5
83. Resolve conflict among group members	1	2	3	4	5
84. Assist with group members' feedback to each other	1	2	3	4	5
85. Determine group counseling termination criteria	1	2	3	4	5
86. Self-evaluate group counseling effectiveness	1	2	3	4	5
87. Use"structured" activities during group counseling	1	2	3	4	5
88. Use leader-centered group counseling leadership techniques	1	2	3	4	5
89. Use group-centered group counseling leadership techniques	1	2	3	4	5
90. Use laissez-faire group counseling leadership techniques	1	2	3	4	5
91. Evaluate client's occupational skills	1	2	3	4	5
92. Evaluate client's educational preparations	1	2	3	4	5
93. Facilitate client's development of decision-making skills	1	2	3	4	5
94. Facilitate clients development of job-search skills	1	2	3	4	5
95. Provide group vocational counseling	1	2	3	4	5
96. Provide out-placement counseling	1	2	3	4	5
97. Use occupational information	1	2	3	4	5
98. Use computerized career counseling resources	1	2	3	4	5
99. Use career resources library	1	2	3	4	5
101. Use print and other media in career counseling	1	2	3	4	5
102. Provide career counseling for children	1	2	3	4	5
103. Provide career counseling for adolescents	1	2	3	4	5
104. Provide career counseling for adults	1	2	3	4	5
105. Provide career counseling for older adults	1	2	3	4	5
106. Provide career counseling for persons with disabilities	1	2	3	4	5
107. Select appraisal instruments/techniques for counseling	1	2	3	4	5
108. Use test results for client decision-making	1	2	3	4	5
109. Assist client in understanding test results	1	2	3	4	5
110. Use test/inventory results for intervention selections	1	2	3	4	5
111. Use aptitude tests	1	2	3	4	5
112. Use achievement tests	1	2	3	4	5
113. Use interest inventories	1	2	3	4	5
114. Use self-report personality inventories	1	2	3	4	5
115. Use intelligence tests	1	2	3	4	5
116. Use non-test appraisal techniques Engage in needs assessments	1	2	3	4	5
117. Engage in needs assessment	1	2	3	4	5
118. Engage in counseling process research	1	2	3	4	5
119. Engage in counseling outcome research	1	2	3	4	5
120. Engage in field/observational research	1	2	3	4	5
121. Engage in experimental/laboratory research	1	2	3	4	5

QUESTIONS CONTINUE ON BACK

Use #2 pencil

RESPONSE FORM I

FREQUENCY

	NEVER 1	RARELY 2	OCCASIONALLY 3	FREQUENTLY 4	ROUTINELY 5
122. Engage in formative evaluation of counseling program					
123. Engage in summative evaluation of counseling program					
124. Engage in data analyses					
125. Collaborate in research with other professionals					
126. Develop appraisal instrument/technique					
127. Evaluate computer software					
128. Provide expert witness testimony					
129. Participate in professional organization activities					
130. Participate in continuing education/skill enhancement					
131. Write for publication					
132. Write communication for non-counseling, professional activities					
133. Review ethical standards					
134. Supervise counselor trainees					
135. Read current professional literature					
136. Review legal statutes and regulations					
137. Assess programmatic needs					
138. Establish programmatic service goals					
139. Participate in staffing decision-making processes					
140. Allocate financial resources for counseling program					
141. Administer counseling program					
142. Use computers for program data management					
143. Conduct fund-raising activities for program development/maintenance					
144. Develop program-related reports					
145. Correspond orally with others to maintain communication					
146. Write to other professionals to maintain communication					
147. Evaluate counselors' performance					
148. Provide counselor skill-development training					
149. Serve as liaison with other agencies					
150. Engage in professional/community public relations					
151. Conduct community outreach					
152. Supervise staff					

DO NOT WRITE IN THIS AREA

DO NOT WRITE IN THIS AREA

Use #2 pencil

WORK BEHAVIOR STUDY
RESPONSE FORM II

IMPORTANCE

CRITICALLY IMPORTANT 5
VERY IMPORTANT 4
MODERATELY IMPORTANT 3
OF LITTLE IMPORTANCE 2
OF NO IMPORTANCE 1

	1	2	3	4	5
1. Obtain client's informed consent prior to counseling	1	2	3	4	5
2. Evaluate existing (pre-counseling) client data	1	2	3	4	5
3. Develop comprehensive treatment plans	1	2	3	4	5
4. Assess psychosocial needs	1	2	3	4	5
5. Assess potential for client to harm self/others	1	2	3	4	5
6. Clarify client's support systems	1	2	3	4	5
7. Systematically observe client behaviors	1	2	3	4	5
8. Assist with client's evaluation of counseling	1	2	3	4	5
9. Self-evaluate counseling effectiveness	1	2	3	4	5
10. Maintain case notes, records, and/or files	1	2	3	4	5
11. Conduct former client follow-up activities	1	2	3	4	5
12. Conduct pre-counseling diagnostic interview	1	2	3	4	5
13. Establish counseling goals	1	2	3	4	5
14. Analyze cost-benefit of treatment alternatives	1	2	3	4	5
15. Determine DSMIII-R classification	1	2	3	4	5
16. Evaluate extent of client's psychological dysfunction	1	2	3	4	5
17. Reframe client's problem	1	2	3	4	5
18. Use computerized "counseling" software	1	2	3	4	5
19. Counsel short-term (less than 6 sessions)	1	2	3	4	5
20. Counsel long-term (6 sessions or longer)	1	2	3	4	5
21. Interview client's significant others	1	2	3	4	5
22. Research use of a specific counseling intervention	1	2	3	4	5
23. Counsel children	1	2	3	4	5
24. Counsel adolescents	1	2	3	4	5
25. Counsel adults	1	2	3	4	5
26. Counsel older persons	1	2	3	4	5
27. Counsel persons in crisis	1	2	3	4	5
28. Counsel clients concerning substance use/abuse	1	2	3	4	5
39. Counsel clients concerning personal change	1	2	3	4	5
30. Counsel clients concerning physical abuse	1	2	3	4	5
31. Counsel clients concerning lifestyle change	1	2	3	4	5
32. Counsel clients concerning personality change	1	2	3	4	5
33. Counsel clients concerning sexual abuse	1	2	3	4	5
34. Use "active listening" skills	1	2	3	4	5
35. Use affective-oriented counseling techniques	1	2	3	4	5
36. Use behavioral-oriented counseling techniques	1	2	3	4	5
37. Use cognitive-oriented counseling techniques	1	2	3	4	5
38. Use brief psychotherapy techniques	1	2	3	4	5
39. Use media resources in counseling	1	2	3	4	5
40. Inform client about human growth and development	1	2	3	4	5

QUESTIONS CONTINUE ON THE BACK

Printed in U.S.A. Trans-Optic® by NCS MP16424 333231

Use #2 pencil

RESPONSE FORM II

IMPORTANCE

CRITICALLY IMPORTANT 5
VERY IMPORTANT 4
MODERATELY IMPORTANT 3
OF LITTLE IMPORTANCE 2
OF NO IMPORTANCE 1

	1	2	3	4	5
41. Inform client about ethical standards and practice	1	2	3	4	5
42. Inform client about legal aspects of counseling	1	2	3	4	5
43. Evaluate need for client referral	1	2	3	4	5
44. Evaluate client's movement toward counseling goals	1	2	3	4	5
45. Clarify counselor/client role	1	2	3	4	5
46. Clarify client's moral/spiritual issues	1	2	3	4	5
47. Identify source-of-problem alternatives	1	2	3	4	5
48. Identify client's non-counseling resources	1	2	3	4	5
49. Provide human development education	1	2	3	4	5
50. Provide career/vocational education	1	2	3	4	5
51. Provide mental health enhancement training/education	1	2	3	4	5
52. Prepare developmental/preventative media	1	2	3	4	5
53. Conduct prevention-oriented developmental activities	1	2	3	4	5
54. Conduct self-development training for non-clients	1	2	3	4	5
55. Provide multicultural training/education	1	2	3	4	5
56. Participate in case conferences	1	2	3	4	5
57. Provide consultation services for organizational development	1	2	3	4	5
58. Provide consultation services for human relationships development	1	2	3	4	5
69. Provide consultation services for interpersonal skills training	1	2	3	4	5
60. Provide consultation services for human resource needs evaluation	1	2	3	4	5
61. Provide consultation services for ethical or legal dilemmas	1	2	3	4	5
62. Provide consultation services for professional skill development	1	2	3	4	5
63. Inform family members of family counseling guidelines and goals	1	2	3	4	5
64. Inform family of family dynamics/roles	1	2	3	4	5
65. Clarify familial behavior norms	1	2	3	4	5
66. Clarify family counseling goals	1	2	3	4	5
67. Develop family conflict resolution strategies	1	2	3	4	5
68. Use the following family counseling techniques: Multi-generational	1	2	3	4	5
79. Use the following family counseling techniques: Structural	1	2	3	4	5
70. Use the following family counseling techniques: Strategic	1	2	3	4	5
71. Use the following family counseling techniques: Behavioral	1	2	3	4	5
72. Counsel concerning pre-marriage	1	2	3	4	5
73. Counsel concerning divorce	1	2	3	4	5
74. Counsel concerning divorce-conflict reduction	1	2	3	4	5
75. Counsel concerning human sexuality	1	2	3	4	5
76. Counsel concerning marriage enrichment	1	2	3	4	5
77. Counsel concerning family change	1	2	3	4	5
78. Counsel concerning family member interaction	1	2	3	4	5
79. Inform clients of group counseling guidelines and goals	1	2	3	4	5
80. Systematically observe group members' behaviors	1	2	3	4	5

DO NOT WRITE IN THIS AREA

Use #2 pencil

RESPONSE FORM II

IMPORTANCE

CRITICALLY IMPORTANT 5
VERY IMPORTANT 4
MODERATELY IMPORTANT 3
OF LITTLE IMPORTANCE 2
OF NO IMPORTANCE 1

Item	1	2	3	4	5
81. Identify harmful group-member behaviors	1	2	3	4	5
82. Evaluate progress toward group goals	1	2	3	4	5
83. Resolve conflict among group members	1	2	3	4	5
84. Assist with group members' feedback to each other	1	2	3	4	5
85. Determine group counseling termination criteria	1	2	3	4	5
86. Self-evaluate group counseling effectiveness	1	2	3	4	5
87. Use"structured" activities during group counseling	1	2	3	4	5
88. Use leader-centered group counseling leadership techniques	1	2	3	4	5
89. Use group-centered group counseling leadership techniques	1	2	3	4	5
90. Use laissez-faire group counseling leadership techniques	1	2	3	4	5
91. Evaluate client's occupational skills	1	2	3	4	5
92. Evaluate client's educational preparations	1	2	3	4	5
93. Facilitate client's development of decision-making skills	1	2	3	4	5
94. Facilitate clients development of job-search skills	1	2	3	4	5
95. Provide group vocational counseling	1	2	3	4	5
96. Provide out-placement counseling	1	2	3	4	5
97. Use occupational information	1	2	3	4	5
98. Use computerized career counseling resources	1	2	3	4	5
99. Use career resources library	1	2	3	4	5
101. Use print and other media in career counseling	1	2	3	4	5
102. Provide career counseling for children	1	2	3	4	5
103. Provide career counseling for adolescents	1	2	3	4	5
104. Provide career counseling for adults	1	2	3	4	5
105. Provide career counseling for older adults	1	2	3	4	5
106. Provide career counseling for persons with disabilities	1	2	3	4	5
107. Select appraisal instruments/techniques for counseling	1	2	3	4	5
108. Use test results for client decision-making	1	2	3	4	5
109. Assist client in understanding test results	1	2	3	4	5
110. Use test/inventory results for intervention selections	1	2	3	4	5
111. Use aptitude tests	1	2	3	4	5
112. Use achievement tests	1	2	3	4	5
113. Use interest inventories	1	2	3	4	5
114. Use self-report personality inventories	1	2	3	4	5
115. Use intelligence tests	1	2	3	4	5
116. Use non-test appraisal techniques Engage in needs assessments	1	2	3	4	5
117. Engage in needs assessment	1	2	3	4	5
118. Engage in counseling process research	1	2	3	4	5
119. Engage in counseling outcome research	1	2	3	4	5
120. Engage in field/observational research	1	2	3	4	5
121. Engage in experimental/laboratory research	1	2	3	4	5

QUESTIONS CONTINUE ON THE BACK

Use #2 pencil

RESPONSE FORM II

IMPORTANCE

5 CRITICALLY IMPORTANT
4 VERY IMPORTANT
3 MODERATELY IMPORTANT
2 OF LITTLE IMPORTANCE
1 OF NO IMPORTANCE

122. Engage in formative evaluation of counseling program
123. Engage in summative evaluation of counseling program
124. Engage in data analyses
125. Collaborate in research with other professionals
126. Develop appraisal instrument/technique
127. Evaluate computer software
128. Provide expert witness testimony
129. Participate in professional organization activities
130. Participate in continuing education/skill enhancement
131. Write for publication
132. Write communication for non-counseling, professional activities
133. Review ethical standards
134. Supervise counselor trainees
135. Read current professional literature
136. Review legal statutes and regulations
137. Assess programmatic needs
138. Establish programmatic service goals
139. Participate in staffing decision-making processes
140. Allocate financial resources for counseling program
141. Administer counseling program
142. Use computers for program data management
143. Conduct fund-raising activities for program development/maintenance
144. Develop program-related reports
145. Correspond orally with others to maintain communication
146. Write to other professionals to maintain communication
147. Evaluate counselors' performance
148. Provide counselor skill-development training
149. Serve as liaison with other agencies
150. Engage in professional/community public relations
151. Conduct community outreach
152. Supervise staff
153. Please indicate your gender: (1) Male, or (2) Female
154. Please indicate all licensure(s): (1) Professional counselor (or equivalent title), (2) Psychologist, (3) Marriage/Family counselor, (4) School Certification, or (5) CCMHC
155. In addition to NCC, what certifications do you hold: (1) NCCC, (2) AAMFT, (3) CCMHC, (4) CRC, (5) School Counselor

APPENDIX E

Work Behavior Statement Response Choice Frequency Data for FREQUENCY Ratings

Item	Response Choice[a] 1	2	3	4	5
1. Obtain client's informed consent prior to counseling	83	112	53	81	386
2. Evaluate existing (precounseling) client data	15	69	116	170	350
3. Develop comprehensive treatment plans	61	109	146	175	226
4. Assess psychosocial needs	23	48	127	210	309
5. Assess potential for client to harm self/others	23	71	104	113	411
6. Clarify client's support systems	9	20	77	230	387
7. Systematically observe client behaviors	15	36	106	172	392
8. Assist with client's evaluation of counseling	39	110	153	219	194
9. Self-evaluate counseling effectiveness	11	14	88	235	365
10. Maintain case notes, records, and/or files	10	42	53	76	535
11. Conduct former client follow-up activities	70	222	238	119	71
12. Conduct precounseling diagnostic interview	85	159	144	141	190
13. Establish counseling goals	16	17	51	189	447
14. Analyze cost-benefit of treatment alternatives	203	179	144	108	81
15. Determine DSM-III-R classification	250	121	91	85	165
16. Evaluate extent of client's psychological dysfunction	83	104	101	159	264
17. Reframe client's problem	23	45	113	266	268
18. Use computerized "counseling" software	413	127	80	56	37
19. Counsel short-term (less than 6 sessions)	28	89	202	223	177
20. Counsel long-term (6 sessions or longer)	44	88	149	250	186
21. Interview client's significant others	67	160	256	181	57
22. Research use of a specific counseling intervention	90	190	250	148	35
23. Counsel children	217	161	106	72	163
24. Counsel adolescents	55	123	152	146	243
25. Counsel adults	16	45	100	202	358
26. Counselor older persons	143	185	191	127	73
27. Counsel persons in crisis	16	58	204	272	166
28. Counsel clients concerning substance use/abuse	67	137	230	177	103
29. Counsel clients concerning personal change	16	18	90	273	321
30. Counsel clients concerning physical abuse	57	141	269	171	78
31. Counsel clients concerning life-style change	23	85	185	258	170
32. Counsel clients concerning personality change	54	141	246	179	99
33. Counsel clients concerning sexual abuse	71	167	234	157	92
34. Use "active listening" skills	0	8	17	106	585
35. Use affective-oriented counseling techniques	9	43	132	269	261
36. Use behavioral-oriented counseling techniques	6	48	182	287	197
37. Use cognitive-oriented counseling techniques	10	39	156	293	221
38. Use brief psychotherapy techniques	81	137	212	180	98
39. Use media resources in counseling	66	200	239	151	62
40. Inform client about human growth and development	7	62	186	288	177

Item	Response Choice[a] 1	2	3	4	5
41. Inform client about ethical standards and practice	20	102	180	153	262
42. Inform client about legal aspects of counseling	50	186	190	142	147
43. Evaluate need for client referral	11	22	135	221	327
44. Evaluate client's movement toward counseling goals	14	13	79	222	386
45. Clarify counselor/client roles	14	50	159	227	263
46. Clarify client's moral/spiritual issues	58	158	219	179	96
47. Identify source-of-problem alternatives	14	31	158	302	201
48. Identify client's noncounseling resources	10	32	165	275	233
49. Provide human development education	25	94	235	245	111
50. Provide career/vocational education	43	159	184	164	165
51. Provide mental health enhancement training/education	80	121	235	181	101
52. Prepare developmental/preventative media	198	206	171	97	42
53. Conduct prevention-oriented developmental activities	103	149	224	157	82
54. Conduct self-development training for nonclients	172	159	218	105	59
55. Provide multicultural training/education	237	216	146	67	52
56. Participate in case conferences	40	122	172	153	228
57. Provide consultation services for organizational development	190	177	177	123	49
58. Provide consultation services for human relationships development	142	169	217	128	59
59. Provide consultation services for interpersonal skills training	133	140	246	130	62
60. Provide consultation services for human resource needs evaluation	221	199	182	81	32
61. Provide consultation services for ethical or legal dilemmas	294	217	126	56	24
62. Provide consultation services for professional skill development	158	144	224	133	55
63. Inform family members of family counseling guidelines and goals	105	143	187	160	122
64. Inform family of family dynamics/roles	104	134	194	167	117
65. Clarify familial behavior norms	104	150	185	167	108
66. Clarify family counseling goals	140	136	167	146	126
67. Develop family conflict resoluation strategies	119	135	166	168	117
68. Use the following family counseling techniques: multigenerational	225	172	169	86	54
69. Use the following family counseling techniques: structural	208	155	178	120	45
70. Use the following family counseling techniques: strategic	217	171	170	106	43
71. Use the following family counseling techniques: behavioral	178	140	176	150	65
72. Counsel concerning premarriage	265	226	148	50	22
73. Counsel concerning divorce	150	131	219	152	58
74. Counsel concerning divorce-conflict reduction	171	151	215	122	46
75. Counsel concerning human sexuality	138	140	243	140	46
76. Counsel concerning marriage enrichment	239	146	169	108	43

Item	Response Choice[a] 1	2	3	4	5
77. Counsel concerning family change	84	83	250	210	83
78. Counsel concerning family member interaction	67	75	213	228	124
79. Inform clients of group counseling guidelines and goals	107	89	148	147	219
80. Systematically observe group members' behaviors	112	75	124	154	247
81. Identify harmful group-member behaviors	107	93	151	144	224
82. Evaluate progress toward group goals	113	71	128	187	216
83. Resolve conflict among group members	111	83	201	165	157
84. Assist with group members' feedback to each other	107	74	140	191	207
85. Determine group counseling termination criteria	130	100	144	150	197
86. Self-evaluate group counseling effectiveness	117	71	128	160	242
87. Use "structured" activities during group counseling	114	93	196	176	136
88. Use leader-centered group counseling leadership techniques	116	142	211	172	75
89. Use group-centered group counseling leadership techniques	119	104	194	206	94
90. Use laissez-faire group counseling leadership techniques	244	258	147	48	16
91. Evaluate client's occupational skills	111	167	182	136	127
92. Evaluate client's educational preparations	41	119	178	162	221
93. Facilitate client's development of decision-making skills	15	26	131	303	245
94. Facilitate client's development of job-search skills	103	170	204	127	118
95. Provide group vocational counseling	306	160	113	68	73
96. Provide outplacement counseling	371	137	102	59	44
97. Use occupational information	152	163	130	115	159
98. Use computerized career counseling resources	342	102	93	78	101
99. Use career resources library	263	127	121	97	111
100. --	-	-	-	-	-
101. Use print and other media in career counseling	221	131	122	109	132
102. Provide career counseling for children	446	120	72	44	34
103. Provide career counseling for adolescents	234	134	150	86	116
104. Provide career counseling for adults	202	152	147	103	115
105. Provide career counseling for older adults	352	147	104	57	56
106. Provide career counseling for persons with disabilities	288	169	121	71	70
107. Select appraisal instruments/techniques for counseling	138	136	183	137	117
108. Use test results for client decison making	113	117	189	164	136
109. Assist client in understanding test results	91	86	145	169	227
110. Use test/inventory results for intervention selections	119	141	200	146	108
111. Use aptitude tests	226	169	137	71	114
112. Use achievement tests	234	147	114	97	130
113. Use interest inventories	158	136	158	127	143
114. Use self-report personality inventories	136	145	198	137	106
115. Use intelligence tests	251	168	131	89	74
116. Use nontest appraisal techniques	204	110	159	138	105

Item	Response Choice[a] 1	2	3	4	5
117. Engage in needs assessment	103	128	204	164	119
118. Engage in counseling process research	335	186	117	58	25
119. Engage in counseling outcome research	341	174	126	59	21
120. Engage in field/observational research	383	173	104	42	18
121. Engage in experimental/laboratory research	541	128	30	14	5
122. Engage in formative evaluation of counseling program	203	137	181	110	78
123. Engage in summative evaluation of counseling program	199	134	179	107	84
124. Engage in data analyses	263	161	153	80	52
125. Collaborate in research with other professionals	266	218	122	60	44
126. Develop appraisal instrument/technique	354	177	116	41	22
127. Evaluate computer software	446	136	75	29	19
128. Provide expert witness testimony	51	196	109	33	20
129. Participate in professional organization activities	31	87	185	194	211
130. Participate in continuing education/skill enhancement	14	11	82	243	357
131. Write for publication	332	186	111	47	30
132. Write communication for non-counseling, professional activities	247	160	151	100	48
133. Review ethical standards	123	156	260	112	61
134. Supervise counselor trainees	217	152	154	101	89
135. Read current professional literature	9	23	142	240	294
136. Review legal statutes and regulations	53	172	241	145	100
137. Assess programmatic needs	67	120	192	189	139
138. Establish programmatic service goals	99	127	177	164	135
139. Participate in staffing decision-making processes	90	76	129	171	240
140. Allocate financial resources for counseling program	337	10	87	73	101
141. Administer counseling program	265	75	84	76	209
142. Use computers for program data management	361	96	93	64	93
143. Conduct fund-raising activities for program development maintenance	511	109	55	21	16
144. Develop program-related reports	207	112	166	127	96
145. Correspond orally with others to maintain					
146. Write to other professionals to maintain communication	63	121	195	169	162
147. Evaluate counselors' performance	213	131	138	99	125
148. Provide counselor skill-development training	174	139	177	118	97
149. Serve as liaison with other agencies	88	73	183	189	175
150. Engage in professional/community public relations	67	97	193	184	166
151. Conduct community outreach	141	140	182	139	106
152. Supervise staff	266	113	96	63	166

[a] 1 = never, 2 = rarely, 3 = occasionally, 4 = frequently, and 5 = routinely.

APPENDIX F

Work Behavior Statement Response Choice Frequency Data for IMPORTANCE Ratings

Item	Response Choice[a] 1	2	3	4	5
1. Obtain client's informed consent prior to counseling	94	118	137	167	194
2. Evaluate existing (precounseling) client data	36	100	194	257	123
3. Develop comprehensive treatment plans	45	103	184	238	141
4. Assess psychosocial needs	33	66	165	281	164
5. Assess potential for client to harm self/others	31	56	95	159	366
6. Clarify client's support systems	12	49	145	313	189
7. Systematically observe client behaviors	25	71	176	247	189
8. Assist with client's evaluation of counseling	33	76	206	259	134
9. Self-evaluate counseling effectiveness	31	60	160	245	215
10. Maintain case notes, records, and/or files	39	109	171	178	210
11. Conduct former client follow-up activities	77	188	266	136	43
12. Conduct precounseling diagnostic interview	76	156	218	166	93
13. Establish counseling goals	10	29	122	296	253
14. Analyze cost-benefit of treatment alternatives	160	94	184	179	90
15. Determine DSM-III-R classification	265	188	123	70	54
16. Evaluate extent of client's psycholgocal dysfunction	64	87	137	222	200
17. Reframe client's problem	17	58	190	303	141
18. Use computerized "counseling" software	322	203	114	44	16
19. Counsel short-term (less than 6 sessions)	36	91	222	223	136
20. Counsel long-term (6 sessions or longer	42	91	212	256	104
21. Interview client's significant others	55	154	269	189	44
22. Research use of a specific counseling intervention	173	178	197	128	27
23. Counsel children	185	90	127	118	184
24. Counsel adolescents	63	64	115	197	267
25. Counsel adults	24	33	102	239	305
26. Counselor older persons	112	109	169	184	127
27. Counsel persons in crisis	14	20	78	152	441
28. Counsel clients concerning substance use/abuse	39	63	142	220	236
29. Counsel clients concerning personal change	11	22	87	288	299
30. Counsel clients concerning physical abuse	34	58	126	200	287
31. Counsel clients concerning life-style change	28	41	149	271	218
32. Counsel clients concerning personality change	34	77	168	247	180
33. Counsel clients concerning sexual abuse	37	70	112	190	297
34. Use "active listening" skills	6	14	42	177	469
35. Use affective-oriented counseling techniques	31	57	159	250	206
36. Use behavioral-oriented counseling techniques	31	62	190	268	155
37. Use cognitive-oriented counseling techniques	31	57	169	296	152
38. Use brief psychotherapy techniques	82	121	206	194	101
39. Use media resources in counseling	103	202	233	114	56
40. Inform client about human growth and development	23	79	245	248	115

	Response Choice[a]				
Item	1	2	3	4	5
41. Inform client about ethical standards and practice	51	121	220	182	132
42. Inform client about legal aspects of counseling	65	162	217	162	98
43. Evaluate need for client referral	18	55	157	280	193
44. Evaluate client's movement toward counseling goals	16	22	116	310	239
45. Clarify counselor/client roles	16	46	166	275	199
46. Clarify client's moral/spiritual issues	58	146	245	176	77
47. Identify source-of-problem alternatives	12	42	160	311	173
48. Identify client's noncounseling resources	17	61	214	265	136
49. Provide human development education	39	121	268	194	75
50. Provide career/vocational education	68	142	200	124	164
51. Provide mental health enhancement training/education	84	137	245	170	68
52. Prepare developmental/preventative media	179	215	178	102	29
53. Conduct prevention-oriented developmental activities	91	157	217	176	59
54. Conduct self-development training for nonclients	218	188	176	86	30
55. Provide multicultural training/education	190	198	173	94	48
56. Participate in case conferences	89	147	176	166	123
57. Provide consultation services for organizational development	233	179	147	95	43
58. Provide consultation services for human relationships development	178	139	195	135	50
59. Provide consultation services for interpersonal skills training	163	129	199	159	49
60. Provide consultation services for human resource needs evaluation	205	167	183	107	34
61. Provide consultation services for ethical or legal dilemmas	203	199	175	86	36
62. Provide consultation services for professional skill development	192	175	165	122	41
63. Inform family members of family counseling guidelines and goals	82	118	203	198	100
64. Inform family of family dynamics/roles	81	113	184	238	85
65. Clarify familial behavior norms	75	108	204	232	82
66. Clarify family counseling goals	96	93	148	234	126
67. Develop family conflict resolution strategies	75	66	136	252	167
68. Use the following family counseling techniques: multigenerational	185	168	175	123	46
69. Use the following family counseling techniques: structural	175	162	192	129	39
70. Use the following family counseling techniques: strategic	173	164	186	130	41
71. Use the following family counseling techniques: behavioral	160	129	173	172	63
72. Counsel concerning premarriage	186	166	182	118	50
73. Counsel concerning divorce	104	92	175	229	103
74. Counsel concerning divorce-conflict reduction 109	87	166	217	116	
75. Counsel concerning human sexuality	88	113	184	213	97
76. Counsel concerning marriage enrichment	166	130	148	179	72
77. Counsel concerning family change	56	63	174	271	134

Item	Response Choice[a] 1	2	3	4	5
78. Counsel concerning family member interaction	50	49	151	288	157
79. Inform clients of group counseling guidelines and goals	91	77	165	207	157
80. Systematically observe group members' behaviors	107	97	166	187	140
81. Identify harmful group-member behaviors	81	51	124	207	240
82. Evaluate progress toward group goals	87	53	128	282	151
83. Resolve conflict among group members	77	41	127	258	200
84. Assist with group members' feedback to each other	78	42	123	272	185
85. Determine group counseling termination criteria	100	67	166	241	125
86. Self-evaluate group counseling effectiveness	95	74	184	222	123
87. Use "structured" activities during group counseling	91	84	244	214	66
88. Use leader-centered group counseling leadership techniques	95	101	237	209	54
89. Use group-centered group counseling leadership techniques	95	76	231	234	59
90. Use laissez-faire group counseling leadership techniques	194	227	176	83	14
91. Evaluate client's occupational skills	103	169	184	118	132
92. Evaluate client's educational preparations	64	120	182	163	172
93. Facilitate client's development of decision-making skills	23	29	140	311	201
94. Facilitate client's development of job-search skills	100	141	195	144	121
95. Provide group vocational counseling	202	179	140	97	85
96. Provide outplacement counseling	252	157	134	98	59
97. Use occupational information	146	149	151	114	142
98. Use computerized career counseling resources	254	143	133	103	71
99. Use career resources library	224	135	139	116	90
100. --	-	-	-	-	-
101. Use print and other media in career counseling	193	140	156	126	87
102. Provide career counseling for children	327	174	101	62	37
103. Provide career counseling for adolescents	168	115	146	147	126
104. Provide career counseling for adults	163	121	128	138	149
105. Provide career counseling for older adults	228	161	127	109	78
106. Provide career counseling for persons with disabilities	188	123	132	145	111
107. Select appraisal instruments/techniques for counseling	136	124	188	152	101
108. Use test results for client decision making	89	115	205	177	121
109. Assist client in understanding test results	72	61	142	216	211
110. Use test/inventory results for intervention selections	100	124	211	169	99
111. Use aptitude tests	157	162	163	112	110
112. Use achievement tests	164	152	159	138	92
113. Use interest inventories	119	100	187	178	119
114. Use self-report personality inventories	98	127	199	192	88
115. Use intelligence tests	173	176	164	116	71
116. Use nontest appraisal techniques	173	127	181	148	69

Item	Response Choice[a] 1	2	3	4	5
117. Engage in needs assessment	123	97	208	179	91
118. Engage in counseling process research	318	171	138	56	20
119. Engage in counseling outcome research	311	172	139	55	23
120. Engage in field/observational research	349	166	125	47	14
121. Engage in experimental/laboratory research	420	162	91	18	11
122. Engage in formative evaluation of counseling program	227	141	170	123	43
123. Engage in summative evaluation of counseling program	231	135	169	125	40
124. Engage in data analyses	312	151	142	69	25
125. Collaborate in research with other professionals	283	191	131	64	31
126. Develop appraisal instrument/technique	319	188	136	38	20
127. Evaluate computer software	369	159	119	34	14
128. Provide expert witness testimony	226	159	160	104	49
129. Participate in professional organization activities	129	148	179	148	96
130. Participate in continuing education/skill enhancement	69	79	135	221	190
131. Write for publication	307	194	123	53	21
132. Write communication for noncounseling, professional activities	301	179	139	62	17
133. Review ethical standards	136	145	189	158	73
134. Supervise counselor trainees	257	158	131	104	51
135. Read current professional literature	70	86	199	179	167
136. Review legal statutes and regulations	111	144	196	162	89
137. Assess programmatic needs	161	132	190	153	59
138. Establish programmatic service goals	164	137	199	140	60
139. Participate in staffing decision-making processes	169	115	154	158	101
140. Allocate financial resources for counseling program	270	159	128	99	42
141. Administer counseling program	245	119	119	124	93
142. Use computers for program data management	338	143	135	53	29
143. Conduct fund-raising activities for program development/maintenance	417	154	86	29	10
144. Develop program-related reports	299	160	144	62	33
145. Correspond orally with others to maintain communication	101	75	175	199	145
146. Write to other professionals to maintain communication	150	120	221	131	73
147. Evaluate counselors' performance	189	115	155	157	78
148. Provide counselor skill development training	196	138	165	120	76
149. Serve as liaison with other agencies	106	99	191	187	108
150. Engage in professional/community public relations	134	126	193	168	77
151. Conduct community outreach	155	142	203	132	63
152. Supervise staff	277	127	117	79	74

[a] 1 = never, 2 = rarely, 3 = occasionally, 4 = frequently, and 5 = routinely.

APPENDIX G

General ANOVA *F* Tests for Significant Differences in FREQUENCY Response Means Based on Selected Demographic Characteristics

Item	Gender	Degree Level	Job Setting	Licensures	Certifications
1.	3.63	0.24	41.25*	1.48	14.97*
			ED= 3.50		NC= 3.92
			CM= 4.16		OC= 3.36
2.	2.26	1.58	14.42*	0.93	0.36
			ED= 3.93		
			CM= 4.23		
3.	0.51	0.43	72.68*	6.23	7.92*
			ED= 3.20		NC= 3.62
			CM= 3.97		OC= 3.27
4.	0.00	1.60	48.66*	1.06	11.96*
			ED= 3.78		NC= 4.10
			CM= 4.31		OC= 3.71
5.	0.07	2.13	30.51*	0.00	9.51*
			ED= 3.93		NC= 4.20
			CM= 4.37		OC= 3.85
6.	1.52	0.48	17.58*	1.84	10.27*
			ED= 4.23		NC= 4.38
			CM= 4.67		OC= 4.13
7.	0.05	0.16	36.64*	6.01	3.61
			ED= 4.04		
			CM= 4.46		
8.	0.01	6.05	27.11*	0.06	13.93*
			ED= 3.39		NC= 3.66
			CM= 3.82		OC= 3.24
9.	0.84	0.03	2.46	1.56	2.33
10.	1.88	2.99*	38.62*	3.65	0.46
		EL= 4.58	ED= 4.33		
		DL= 4.30	CM= 4.74		
11.	0.29	1.42	0.91	2.35	6.60
12.	0.34	1.32	32.48*	1.69	7.97*
			ED= 3.02		NC= 3.34
			CM= 3.56		OC= 2.97
13.	4.16	0.23	8.53*	2.36	5.77
			ED= 4.37		
			CM= 4.52		

Item	Gender	Degree Level	Job Setting	Licensures	Certifications
14.	0.00	2.89	38.89*	1.11	7.74*
			ED = 2.25		NC = 2.63
			CM = 2.92		OC = 2.23
15.	0.84	5.26	172.06*	3.94	14.23*
			ED = 2.06		NC = 2.83
			CM = 3.47		OC = 2.22
16.	0.42	7.01	84.55*	2.38	17.63*
			ED = 3.17		NC = 3.70
			CM = 4.07		OC = 3.12
17.	0.12	2.30	10.40*	1.43	5.87
			ED = 3.88		
			CM = 4.13		
18.	1.64	2.37	14.58*	0.29	0.47
			ED = 2.01		
			CM = 1.65		
19.	1.28	1.29	57.22*	0.13	7.75*
			ED = 3.86		NC = 3.54
			CM = 3.30		OC = 3.84
20.	1.45	0.08	34.89*	2.00	9.14*
			ED = 3.39		NC = 3.69
			CM = 3.89		OC = 3.35
21.	0.11	0.57	1.44	1.09	0.19
22.	0.05	1.92	0.01	3.15	7.81*
					NC = 2.84
					OC = 2.54
23.	2.45	4.16	10.86*	13.15*	7.81*
			ED = 2.86	PC = 2.63	NC = 2.67
			CM = 2.57	OL = 2.84	OC = 2.91
24.	0.22	6.10	37.47*	6.20	19.08*
			ED = 3.81		NC = 3.46
			CM = 3.26		OC = 3.95
25.	1.02	2.04	96.44*	19.91*	30.46*
			ED = 3.85	PC = 4.31	NC = 4.26
			CM = 4.54	OL = 3.97	OC = 3.75
26.	0.67	0.93	44.34*	1.39	12.40*
			ED = 2.41		NC = 2.82
			CM = 3.09		OC = 2.34
27.	2.13	0.04	5.35	0.00	0.28
28.	0.52	3.72	10.26*	1.16	1.73
			ED = 3.05		
			CM = 3.28		
29.	0.10	0.10	10.28*	4.34	7.30*
			ED = 4.12		NC = 4.25
			CM = 4.30		OC = 4.01
30.	7.75*	2.98	15.21*	3.32	1.76
	M = 2.96		ED = 2.99		
	F = 3.18		CM = 3.23		

Item	Gender	Degree Level	Job Setting	Licensures	Certifications
31.	0.00	0.29	50.56*	2.97	26.41*
			ED= 3.40		NC= 3.75
			CM= 3.94		OC= 3.22
32.	0.06	1.07	20.97*	0.58	7.76*
			ED= 3.01		NC= 3.24
			CM= 3.38		OC= 2.91
33.	13.96*	0.18	30.63*	1.61	4.75
	M= 2.83		ED= 2.86		
	F= 3.15		CM= 3.27		
34.	12.28*	0.01	0.10	3.60	2.91
	M= 4.66				
	F= 4.82				
35.	4.71	1.64	0.37	0.02	0.97
36.	0.22	0.42	0.70	0.63	3.76
37.	0.12	4.91	8.60*	2.92	17.68*
			ED= 3.85		NC= 4.02
			CM= 4.04		OC= 3.62
38.	2.51	16.30*	8.82*	0.02	12.45*
		EL= 3.01	ED= 2.98		NC= 3.20
		DL= 3.45	CM= 3.26		OC= 2.75
39.	0.44	1.44	0.62	0.11	0.21
40.	1.38	0.00	2.54	0.11	4.08
41.	0.01	2.63	16.73*	0.15	9.97*
			ED= 3.58		NC= 3.81
			CM= 3.95		OC= 3.47
42.	0.00	2.28	31.57*	0 .51	18.07*
			ED= 2.96		NC= 3.30
			CM= 3.50		OC= 2.82
43.	0.19	2.19	3.61	0.18	1.68
44.	0.21	0.18	20.21*	1.19	9.21*
			ED= 4.21		NC= 4.39
			CM= 4.48		OC= 4.10
45.	0.27	0.54	23.31*	0.08	9.33*
			ED= 3.78		NC= 4.00
			CM= 4.14		OC= 3.69
46.	0.15	2.27	23.93*	0.35	3.03
			ED= 2.93		
			CM= 3.36		
47.	0.02	0.36	0.92	2.44	1.63
48.	0.99	0.92	7.77*	5.40	3.30
			ED= 3.88		
			CM= 4.06		
49.	6.29	1.92	1.29	0.63	0.11
50.	0.34	0.43	33.34*	0.13	4.93
			ED= 3.58		
			CM= 3.08		
51.	3.98	4.34	0.51	0.03	0.64

Item	Gender	Degree Level	Job Setting	Licensures	Certifications
52.	1.43	0.37	9.99*	0.08	2.31
			ED = 2.54		
			CM = 2.25		
53.	4.66	1.02	35.33*	0.68	4.00
			ED = 3.20		
			CM = 2.66		
54.	4.90	5.72	13.53*	0.20	0.26
			ED = 2.76		
			CM = 2.43		
55.	0.36	4.76	21.75*	2.44	2.99
			ED = 2.49		
			CM = 2.03		
56.	0.92	9.07*	12.66*	0.12	0.09
		EL = 3.64	ED = 3.42		
		DL = 3.31	CM = 3.73		
57.	0.29	0.45	4.05	1.19	0.19
58.	0.03	4.69	14.57*	0.19	0.00
			ED = 2.88		
			CM = 2.51		
59.	0.80	5.28	17.13*	0.62	0.08
			ED = 2.97		
			CM = 2.57		
60.	0.05	0.09	10.53*	1.08	0.01
			ED = 2.31		
			CM = 2.13		
61.	0.75	13.03*	2.91	4.99	1.44
		EL = 1.94			
		DL = 2.33			
62.	0.22	6.82	9.30*	3.28	3.63
			ED = 2.84		
			CM = 2.53		
63.	1.26	1.22	25.95*	0.68	0.09
			ED = 2.86		
			CM = 3.32		
64.	0.98	0.56	48.23*	1.05	3.08
			ED = 2.81		
			CM = 3.40		
65.	0.18	2.72	41.47*	0.01	4.81
			ED = 2.77		
			CM = 3.34		
66.	0.00	1.32	61.94*	0.00	6.06
			ED = 2.63		
			CM = 3.37		
67.	0.29	0.31	42.48*	0.00	4.68
			ED = 2.77		
			CM = 3.36		

Item	Gender	Degree Level	Job Setting	Licensures	Certifications
68.	3.36	1.38	24.80*	2.77	3.85
			ED = 2.17		
			CM = 2.65		
69.	0.07	0.01	29.37*	0.58	4.22
			ED = 2.25		
			CM = 2.76		
70.	0.00	0.22	20.25*	0.17	1.79
			ED = 2.20		
			CM = 2.66		
71.	0.64	0.51	10.57*	0.71	3.50
			ED = 2.53		
			CM = 2.88		
72.	1.44	9.56*	5.33	2.02	3.99
		EL = 2.00			
		DL = 2.32			
73.	0.10	6.92*	7.05*	0.21	4.30
		EL = 2.70	ED = 2.65		
		DL = 3.01	CM = 2.91		
74.	0.16	10.54*	12.95*	0.53	7.18*
		EL = 2.52	ED = 2.44		NC = 2.67
		DL = 2.88	CM = 2.80		OC = 2.33
75.	0.15	1.86	8.78*	2.00	1.40
			ED = 2.63		
			CM = 2.87		
76.	0.03	8.12*	48.03*	0.00	9.64*
		EL = 2.31	ED = 2.07		NC = 2.47
		DL = 2.66	CM = 2.75		OC = 2.08
77.	5.23	0.29	16.16*	0.00	1.89
			ED = 3.03		
			CM = 3.35		
78.	2.37	0.05	15.08*	0.08	0.50
			ED = 3.23		
			CM = 3.54		
79.	6.72	1.50	0.15	0.72	1.91
80.	4.90	1.61	0.30	0.00	0.21
81.	0.91	0.28	0.44	0.15	0.33
82.	3.16	0.41	0.10	0.04	1.73
83.	0.02	2.36	0.05	0.09	0.66
84.	0.04	0.56	0.01	0.01	0.50
85.	1.50	0.87	0.25	0.09	1.89
86.	0.06	0.05	0.02	0.72	2.58
87.	0.25	3.28	5.29	0.49	7.94*
					NC = 3.11
					OC = 3.45
88.	0.03	1.33	11.0	0.1	7.36*
			ED = 3.08		NC = 2.87
			CM = 2.75		OC = 3.15
89.	0.58	0.21	0.98	0.01	1.34

Item	Gender	Degree Level	Job Setting	Licensures	Certifications
90.	0.33	0.16	0.19	0.02	1.37
91.	2.17	1.40	0.13	1.91	0.00
92.	0.36	4.53	31.54*	0.52	6.81*
			ED = 3.78		NC = 3.51
			CM = 3.30		OC = 3.77
93.	0.01	3.94	0.28	0.10	1.01
94.	1.22	2.77	0.34	2.20	0.02
95.	0.39	2.19	52.18*	0.03	3.77
			ED = 2.57		
			CM = 1.82		
96.	0.56	0.31	3.60	0.02	0.29
97.	1.12	1.57	35.71*	0.21	2.72
			ED = 3.26		
			CM = 2.60		
98.	2.24	0.00	57.69*	0.49	1.07
			ED = 2.68		
			CM = 1.84		
99.	0.12	0.06	73.14*	0.13	4.41
			ED = 2.98		
			CM = 2.02		
100.	X	X	X	X	X
101.	0.31	1.35	65.17*	0.12	8.73*
			ED = 3.16		NC = 2.64
			CM = 2.21		OC = 3.08
102.	0.89	0.91	80.21*	11.25*	7.66*
			ED = 2.11	PC = 1.62	NC = 1.68
			CM = 1.31	OL = 1.92	OC = 1.99
103.	0.00	4.07	125.55*	10.82*	18.25*
			ED = 3.14	PC = 2.46	NC = 2.49
			CM = 1.98	OL = 2.80	OC = 3.08
104.	5.11	2.52	1.91	2.05	3.71
105.	0.66	0.67	3.37	1.31	1.61
106.	0.79	1.82	7.90*	0.00	1.10
			ED = 2.44		
			CM = 2.05		
107.	2.44	3.05	12.94*	1.36	0.17
			ED = 3.14		
			CM = 2.71		
108.	1.12	0.71	31.94*	0.88	0.24
			ED = 3.40		
			CM = 2.81		
109.	5.33	3.63	41.12*	0.77	3.59
			ED = 3.81		
			CM = 3.12		
110.	1.73	2.61	10.74*	0.01	0.56
			ED = 3.14		
			CM = 2.79		

Item	Gender	Degree Level	Job Setting	Licensures	Certifications
111.	1.35	0.46	62.29*	4.99	11.78*
			ED= 2.95		NC= 2.45
			CM= 2.08		OC= 2.96
112.	0.11	2.99	154.29*	13.25*	24.64*
			ED= 3.24	PC= 2.47	NC= 2.50
			CM= 1.93	OL= 2.88	OC= 3.23
113.	0.35	0.27	57.99*	0.20	4.10
			ED= 3.34		
			CM= 2.49		
114.	1.75	16.06*	6.30	0.30	0.90
		EL= 2.80			
		DL= 3.28			
115.	0.40	0.61	42.00*	9.15*	8.29*
			ED= 2.70	PC= 2.26	NC= 2.32
			CM= 2.04	OL= 2.58	OC= 2.69
116.	2.23	1.72	4.06	0.01	0.09
117.	1.11	0.86	3.15	0.92	0.18
118.	4.72	9.61*	31.55*	0.62	0.18
		EL= 1.89	ED= 2.19		
		DL= 2.23	CM= 1.69		
119.	8.74*	12.01*	25.36*	1.41	0.77
	M= 2.16	EL= 1.87	ED= 2.16		
	F= 1.86	DL= 2.34	CM= 1.70		
120.	8.38*	13.55*	22.20*	0.28	0.05
	M= 1.99	EL= 1.72	ED= 2.00		
	F= 1.72	DL= 2.09	CM= 1.57		
121.	11.19	19.85*	16.19*	0.63	0.25
	M= 1.80	EL= 1.28	ED= 1.46		
	F= 1.28	DL= 1.57	CM= 1.21		
122.	1.53	1.09	63.16*	1.59	2.27
			ED= 3.00		
			CM= 2.16		
123.	1.63	1.39	63.74*	0.30	1.43
			ED= 3.03		
			CM= 2.17		
124.	0.33	9.23*	27.94*	1.42	0.68
		EL= 2.21	ED= 2.55		
		DL= 2.56	CM= 1.98		
125.	4.85	34.63*	32.88*	4.71	0.02
		EL= 2.01	ED= 2.41		
		DL= 2.63	CM= 1.85		
126.	2.62	9.98*	29.82*	0.90	0.20
		EL= 1.80	ED= 2.10		
		DL= 2.12	CM= 1.61		
127.	3.23	2.01	20.47*	2.57	0.00
			ED= 1.83		
			CM= 1.41		

Item	Gender	Degree Level	Job Setting	Licensures	Certifications
128.	1.87	5.26	8.57* ED = 1.73 CM = 1.96	2.01	1.00
129.	3.93	6.34	50.97* ED = 3.94 CM = 3.33	2.07	3.32
130.	10.70* M = 4.18 F = 4.38	0.48	9.79* ED = 4.40 CM = 4.18	2.58	0.14
131.	5.07	125.58* EL = 1.71 DL = 2.79	17.07* ED = 2.06 CM = 1.82	5.08	0.01
132.	1.41	14.18* EL = 2.25 DL = 2.70	15.89* ED = 2.55 CM = 2.12	1.61	0.01
133.	0.12	10.08* EL = 2.69 DL = 3.01	3.38	0.06	0.69
134.	0.19	26.10* EL = 2.44 DL = 3.03	2.11	0.00	8.06* NC = 2.64 OC = 3.82
135.	4.26	4.91	2.62	0.01	0.04
136.	0.30	8.96* EL = 3.03 DL = 3.20	0.00	0.74	2.41
137.	1.24	5.77	19.36* ED = 3.81 CM = 3.06	0.29	1.38
138.	6.14	5.52	20.97* ED = 3.40 CM = 2.88	0.30	0.87
139.	0.05	3.95	1.97	0.03	3.87
140.	0.04	3.24	2.45	0.54	0.02
141.	0.03	0.85	13.04* ED = 3.08 CM = 2.57	0.82	0.88
142.	3.59	0.52	3.15	1.78	0.06
143.	1.97	1.39	1.44	0.02	0.47
144.	0.16	1.60	15.65* ED = 2.95 CM = 2.43	1.41	0.10
145.	2.83	4.87	9.44* ED = 4.41 CM = 4.17	0.06	0.13
146.	1.67	2.93	1.53	0.91	1.87
147.	1.57	11.26* EL = 2.61 DL = 3.05	0.70	0.01	9.94* NC = 2.79 OC = 2.33

Item	Gender	Degree Level	Job Setting	Licensures	Certifications
148.	0.83	32.93*	1.40	1.02	8.49*
		EL = 2.61			NC = 2.83
		DL = 3.25			OC = 2.43
149.	0.51	0.13	16.87*	0.36	0.77
			ED = 3.61		
			CM = 3.17		
150.	8.82*	0.88	13.74*	0.72	0.23
	M = 3.21	ED = 3.56			
	F = 3.48	CM = 3.22			
151.	4.78	0.80	3.52	0.24	1.12
152.	5.98	6.31	8.58*	0.18	7.60*
			ED = 2.50		NC = 2.72
			CM = 2.82		OC = 2.35

* $p < 0.01$.

Note: Item response means are shown following significant *F* values. M = male; F = female; EL = entry level; DL = doctoral level; ED = educational; CM = community; PC = professional counselor; OL = other licensures; NC = NCC only; OC = other certifications.

APPENDIX H

General ANOVA *F* Tests for Significant Differences in IMPORTANCE Response Means Based on Selected Demographic Characteristics

Item	Gender	Degree Level	Job Setting	Licensures	Certifications
1.	0.29	0.00	17.46*	0.99	9.93*
			ED = 3.15		NC = 3.43
			CM = 3.59		OC = 3.01
2.	4.70	1.10	7.79*	1.08	0.00
		ED = 3.36			
		CM = 3.59			
3.	1.36	0.01	2.93	0.00	1.24
4.	0.17	0.21	11.07*	0.35	2.98
			ED = 3.55		
			CM = 3.82		
5.	1.63	0.19	1.57	0.05	2.99
6.	2.81	0.06	0.06	0.34	0.01
7.	1.12	0.45	6.94*	0.30	0.41
			ED = 3.62		
			CM = 3.82		
8.	6.26	4.17	7.36*	1.47	2.68
			ED = 3.45		
			CM = 3.66		
9.	4.18	0.21	2.30	4.11	0.50
10.	5.32	9.52*	8.91	*0.87	0.05
		EL = 3.42	ED = 3.45		
		DL = 3.62	CM = 3.73		
11.	0.03	1.28	2.96	0.67	1.06
12.	0.18	1.21	13.60*	1.76	3.24
			ED = 2.91		
			CM = 3.24		
13.	6.43	2.48	3.49	3.47	4.65
14.	0.00	2.23	13.34*	1.32	1.82
			ED = 2.73		
			CM = 3.15		
15.	2.27	1.40	30.76*	0.10	0.27
			ED = 1.96		
			CM = 2.52		
16.	1.74	2.63	19.30*	2.79	2.88
			ED = 3.38		
			CM = 3.80		
17.	0.07	6.74	1.15	2.40	0.15
		EL = 3.85			
		DL = 3.65			

Item	Gender	Degree Level	Job Setting	Licensures	Certifications
18.	2.12	0.85	22.34*	0.14	2.40
			ED = 2.07		
			CM = 1.70		
19.	2.17	0.19	13.10*	0.05	1.44
			ED = 3.60		
			CM = 3.32		
20.	0.33	1.66	6.61	2.91	2.76
21.	0.10	0.06	0.82	0.19	1.63
22.	2.12	2.23	0.06	0.00	0.09
23.	0.42	0.65	5.02	0.38	0.09
24.	0.08	2.30	28.03*	0.64	13.86*
			ED = 3.97		NC = 3.68
			CM = 3.52		OC = 4.12
25.	0.74	0.07	16.75*	8.78*	8.33*
			ED = 3.94	PC = 3.95	NC = 4.15
			CM = 4.28	OL = 4.20	OC = 3.84
26.	0.96	1.79	19.53*	2.75	6.94*
			ED = 2.91		NC = 3.23
			CM = 3.43		OC = 2.83
27.	0.97	3.44	0.45	1.13	0.50
28.	0.18	0.13	0.42	0.24	1.43
29.	4.21	0.07	1.51	2.19	0.73
30.	3.01	0.52	1.61	0.12	3.85
31.	2.09	2.93	2.94	1.36	1.87
32.	0.16	0.11	0.94	0.49	0.10
33.	4.27	0.05	0.02	0.24	3.11
34.	13.21*	0.58	2.75	0.00	2.96
	M = 4.38				
	F = 4.62				
35.	0.60	1.09	3.55	0.05	0.00
36.	0.04	0.83	0.84	0.63	3.76
37.	1.02	2.63	0.19	0.01	5.80
38.	3.84	13.28*	1.75	0.00	0.60
		EL = 3.49			
		DL = 3.07			
39.	0.00	0.43	12.89*	0.05	22.55*
			ED = 2.89		NC = 2.65
			CM = 2.57		OC = 3.12
40.	0.51	0.14	7.67	3.69	0.84
			ED = 3.59		
			CM = 3.39		
41.	0.06	3.44	9.02*	0.46	0.22
			ED = 3.18		
			CM = 3.48		
42.	0.87	1.23	7.81*	1.12	2.74
			ED = 2.97		
			CM = 3.25		

Item	Gender	Degree Level	Job Setting	Licensures	Certifications
43.	0.99	1.17	0.08	0.56	0.25
44.	1.02	0.22	1.79	1.45	3.48
45.	1.51	0.80	4.33	0.49	0.04
46.	0.62	2.49	5.09	0.02	0.02
47.	0.01	0.90	0.45	0.15	1.41
48.	2.20	0.43	0.17	0.06	3.25
49.	0.38	3.35	5.61	0.26	5.85
50.	0.01	0.02	37.66*	0.02	15.67*
			ED= 3.51		NC= 3.15
			CM= 2.93		OC= 3.64
51.	0.45	2.18	2.05	0.26	0.61
52.	0.05	2.97	17.41*	0.70	9.00*
			ED= 2.57		NC= 2.35
			CM= 2.23		OC= 2.66
53.	0.43	3.92	40.33*	3.11	10.60*
			ED= 3.17		NC= 2.87
			CM= 2.67		OC= 3.19
54.	0.10	4.27	9.94*	3.25	5.29
			ED= 2.43		
			CM= 2.19		
55.	0.00	1.22	23.06*	0.92	6.23
			ED= 2.65		
			CM= 2.22		
56.	0.36	0.15	2.27	1.05	9.90*
					NC= 3.05
					OC= 3.41
57.	1.82	0.06	3.13	1.18	1.25
58.	1.80	0.62	11.94*	0.94	2.68
			ED= 2.79		
			CM= 2.45		
59.	0.70	0.07	9.24*	1.40	1.01
			ED= 2.86		
			CM= 2.57		
60.	2.05	0.00	0.51	2.12	0.20
61.	9.67*	5.24	0.50	2.05	0.03
	M= 2.54				
	F= 2.25				
62.	4.50	2.87	3.77	3.91	0.54
63.	0.35	1.00	9.45*	0.20	0.95
			ED= 3.04		
			CM= 3.31		
64.	0.18	0.10	15.61*	0.63	0.68
			ED= 3.02		
			CM= 3.37		
65.	0.33	2.41	14.18*	0.35	0.00
			ED= 3.05		
			CM= 3.36		

Item	Gender	Degree Level	Job Setting	Licensures	Certifications
66.	0.01	2.26	26.03*	0.06	0.01
			ED= 3.08		
			CM= 3.54		
67.	0.71	2.52	19.71*	0.33	0.14
			ED= 3.35		
			CM= 3.	74	
68.	0.23	3.98	4.60	1.73	0.06
69.	2.98	3.06	5.75	1.29	0.23
70.	2.03	0.69	0.91	1.68	1.46
71.	3.37	0.83	2.96	3.85	2.27
72.	9.00*	7.87*	4.00	0.07	0.24
	M= 2.73	EL= 2.82			
	F= 2.42	DL= 2.47			
73.	0.53	3.23	1.51	1.66	2.47
74.	0.40	4.52	5.28	0.08	1.64
75.	0.04	5.91	0.70	0.13	0.03
76.	2.97	10.65*	38.60*	0.22	11.03*
		EL= 3.15	ED= 2.51		NC= 2.90
		DL= 2.71	CM= 3.14		OC= 2.39
77.	3.70	0.00	4.23	0.11	0.21
78.	4.90	0.15	1.03	0.11	0.25
79.	1.62	1.35	0.50	0.70	0.67
80.	0.14	2.50	0.84	0.18	1.16
81.	2.19	0.36	0.28	0.20	0.02
82.	1.34	0.07	0.04	0.62	0.26
83.	1.30	0.41	0.87	0.14	2.13
84.	0.48	0.88	0.00	0.21	1.04
85.	0.38	0.67	1.38	0.22	0.70
86.	2.26	0.56	0.41	1.01	3.06
87.	0.05	0.52	9.03*	0.55	7.56*
			ED= 3.24		NC= 3.05
			CM= 2.97		OC= 3.38
88.	0.55	0.14	3.78	0.22	4.34
89.	0.21	0.01	4.79	0.27	2.87
90.	1.26	0.05	5.57	0.02	2.30
91.	2.73	0.00	8.64*	0.13	0.40
			ED= 3.13		
			CM= 2.86		
92.	1.10	0.55	53.98*	1.53	8.86*
			ED= 3.68		NC= 3.30
			CM= 3.00		OC= 3.65
93.	0.72	0.13	9.86*	0.00	7.47*
			ED= 4.01		NC= 3.86
			CM= 3.78		OC= 4.09
94.	4.18	0.21	2.30	4.11	0.50
95.	0.18	0.55	44.44*	0.22	1.69
			ED= 2.88		
			CM= 2.17		

Item	Gender	Degree Level	Job Setting	Licensures	Certifications
96.	2.34	5.15	2.40	0.87	0.48
97.	1.96	0.28	25.78*	0.13	3.61
			ED= 3.20		
			CM= 2.63		
98.	3.72	1.16	37.50*	0.13	9.35*
			ED= 2.72		NC= 2.35
			CM= 2.06		OC= 2.74
99.	1.38	0.01	44.51*	0.00	9.79*
			ED= 2.94		NC= 2.51
			CM= 2.18		OC= 2.93
100.	X	X	X	X	X
101.	0.88	0.03	35.58*	0.06	11.42*
			ED= 2.98		NC= 2.60
			CM= 2.31		OC= 3.02
102.	0.65	0.07	45.00*	7.04*	6.24
			ED= 2.30	PC= 2.16	
			CM= 1.68	OL= 1.91	
103.	2.35	0.80	86.85*	8.54*	28.33*
			ED= 3.35	PC= 3.09	NC= 2.79
			CM= 2.41	OL= 2.81	OC= 3.49
104.	8.76*	5.51	0.69	2.15	1.84
	M= 3.27				
	F= 2.85				
105.	5.80	1.72	0.45	1.95	0.84
106.	5.44	0.63	10.83*	0.00	1.59
			ED= 2.99		
			CM= 2.60		
107.	6.03	0.35	11.14*	0.34	1.30
			ED= 3.13		
			CM= 2.72		
108.	8.25*	1.43	17.68*	1.27	2.36
	M= 3.39		ED= 3.38		
	F= 3.08		CM= 2.93		
109.	6.71*	2.70	18.59*	0.34	1.44
	M= 3.82		ED= 3.84		
	F= 3.53		CM= 3.36		
110.	10.56*	3.04	14.95*	0.20	0.42
	M= 3.28		ED= 3.24		
	F= 2.95		CM= 2.84		
111.	5.12	0.03	44.45*	1.93	3.95
			ED= 3.13		
			CM= 2.39		
112.	3.00	0.09	97.47*	6.10	12.72*
			ED= 3.23		NC= 2.69
			CM= 2.23		OC= 3.15
113.	7.83*	1.80	40.66*	0.32	1.99
	M= 3.32		ED= 3.42		
	F= 3.01		CM= 2.75		

Item	Gender	Degree Level	Job Setting	Licensures	Certifications
114.	1.96	4.45	11.63*	0.13	1.88
			ED = 3.21		
			CM = 2.90		
115.	1.84	0.07	24.82*	5.85	1.15
			ED = 2.85		
			CM = 2.34		
116.	4.02	1.00	1.26	0.10	0.37
117.	2.89	0.94	0.25	0.00	0.23
118.	7.84*	2.25	7.21*	2.09	1.02
	M = 2.18		ED = 2.10		
	F = 1.89		CM = 1.86		
119.	7.91*	1.99	8.62*	0.33	0.56
	M = 2.21		ED = 2.13		
	F = 1.91		CM = 1.88		
120.	10.09*	1.41	4.80	0.71	0.58
	M = 2.08				
	F = 1.77				
121.	12.15*	5.50	2.01	1.22	0.07
	M = 1.82				
	F = 1.53				
122.	0.00	0.18	15.30*	0.32	3.78
			ED = 2.63		
			CM = 2.25		
123.	0.58	0.00	11.57*	0.71	4.77
			ED = 2.60		
			CM = 2.27		
124.	4.01	0.02	4.45	2.10	3.02
125.	6.50	5.01	3.31	1.66	3.02
126.	4.18	0.02	5.20	2.62	2.46
127.	1.51	0.30	25.84*	4.22	0.78
			ED = 1.99		
			CM = 1.58		
128.	1.63	0.23	14.64*	0.11	0.01
			ED = 2.24		
			CM = 2.62		
129.	0.60	0.28	3.61	0.00	6.58
130.	0.05	0.79	0.07	1.65	0.20
131.	1.22	14.01*	0.18	0.07	0.55
		EL = 2.29			
		DL = 1.90			
132.	2.79	1.51	1.44	0.26	1.14
133.	0.08	0.22	0.50	0.70	0.69
134.	4.34	4.09	0.76	0.25	0.16
135.	0.01	2.50	0.28	1.02	2.20
136.	0.39	0.91	1.54	0.18	0.01
137.	0.78	0.49	9.64*	0.06	3.47
			ED = 2.88		
			CM = 2.58		

Item	Gender	Degree Level	Job Setting	Licensures	Certifications
138.	0.03	1.20	8.53*	0.40	3.25
			ED = 2.84		
			CM = 2.56		
139.	1.89	0.78	1.40	0.79	0.99
140.	3.09	7.16*	3.76	0.01	1.83
		EL = 2.50			
		DL = 2.20			
141.	0.85	1.36	16.15*	0.04	11.36*
			ED = 2.78		NC = 2.49
			CM = 2.34		OC = 2.93
142.	11.47*	2.95	12.34*	4.68	16.42*
	M = 2.22		ED = 2.14		NC = 1.90
	F = 1.87		CM = 1.80		OC = 2.33
143.	2.98	0.03	0.18	1.08	0.77
144.	1.21	0.01	0.80	0.37	3.83
145.	0.66	0.26	0.09	0.01	6.94*
					NC = 3.25
					OC = 3.54
146.	0.00	0.01	0.95	0.01	5.16
147.	4.51	6.85*	0.09	0.00	0.02
		EL = 2.97			
		DL = 2.68			
148.	3.37	3.28	0.66	0.46	0.24
149.	0.23	3.71	1.57	0.32	9.27*
					NC = 3.06
					OC = 3.41
150.	1.59	1.63	1.76	0.04	10.60*
					NC = 2.82
					OC = 3.19
151.	0.01	1.50	0.43	1.26	4.33
152.	2.96	0.40	8.80*	1.30	0.24
			ED = 2.20		
			CM = 2.48		

* $p < .01$

Note: item response means are shown following significant *F* values. M = male; F = female; EL = entry level; DL = doctoral level; ED = educational; CM = community; PC = professional counselor; OL = other licensures; NC = NCC only; OC = other certifications.

APPENDIX I

Initial Principal Factors Factor Analysis of FREQUENCY Responses: Orthogonal Transformation Using Varimax Rotation, Retaining Factors With Eigenvalues Greater Than 1

Factors

Item	I	II	III	IV	V	VI	VII	VIII	IX	X
1.	-09	53	05	09	15	-08	05	-12	-21	00
2.	08	49	00	12	14	00	-04	-23	-13	26
3.	-09	62	07	10	23	-01	03	02	-23	04
4.	-15	69	10	04	16	-02	06	24	-08	06
5.	-20	56	16	06	23	-03	-01	26	-04	07
6.	-06	65	14	06	21	-01	-07	12	10	07
7.	-11	58	13	00	17	-04	04	12	-02	04
8.	-06	58	08	03	16	02	22	19	04	-12
9.	00	61	09	-03	00	01	09	12	24	-03
10.	-03	46	03	06	06	-14	-13	-13	-02	17
11.	25	21	17	10	25	19	07	-13	05	03
12.	-01	50	08	05	13	01	12	02	-17	16
13.	04	61	18	-01	23	07	-06	-22	-01	02
14.	-04	50	00	09	10	01	07	17	-17	-06
15.	-29	47	04	-03	28	-17	03	24	-33	02
16.	-22	59	08	-03	23	-09	06	25	-18	01
17.	-05	53	16	03	17	06	-01	17	10	-04
18.	46	-03	-03	17	-03	-04	13	06	-04	06
19.	33	00	02	06	-15	01	-06	07	44	09
20.	-23	49	17	-06	19	-06	-05	15	-06	15
21.	-18	33	07	09	48	-01	-01	08	16	34
22.	-06	33	12	05	23	12	44	-03	05	-02
23.	-24	09	14	-03	45	18	04	-15	20	40
24.	16	-06	15	02	33	-04	-06	08	49	29
25.	12	53	-07	-03	-03	-11	-09	32	-16	-27
26.	23	35	-10	-06	09	01	03	27	-35	-19
27.	-02	34	12	09	14	15	-19	30	09	24
28.	-08	19	23	11	22	13	-23	28	-05	22
29.	01	53	18	00	03	10	-16	26	15	01
30.	-17	28	25	06	30	14	-20	31	-05	23
31.	17	48	01	-01	00	12	-13	37	-17	-17
32.	-04	37	19	-10	11	13	-03	43	-07	09
33.	-26	29	23	06	30	06	-19	37	-05	22
34.	00	33	09	02	-06	06	-04	02	32	-02
35.	-12	33	22	-03	09	13	05	09	22	02
36.	03	40	04	-02	05	18	04	-01	16	22
37.	-07	47	04	-03	03	03	04	16	22	11

Factors

Item	I	II	III	IV	V	VI	VII	VIII	IX	X
38.	-14	38	11	-04	11	17	08	28	08	04
39.	16	19	13	09	04	13	06	-04	21	04
40.	00	40	17	-04	15	19	06	19	35	-17
41.	01	52	08	04	19	14	07	-08	-11	-14
42.	-02	47	03	11	16	13	01	03	-23	-05
43.	11	56	11	09	08	14	-15	-09	06	03
44.	-04	72	09	02	11	09	-03	01	09	-05
45.	07	64	03	05	05	02	08	13	14	-11
46.	-12	43	13	-02	23	08	02	43	03	-14
47.	07	50	20	02	11	16	-10	13	23	01
48.	12	51	12	11	15	12	-17	08	19	-02
49.	05	25	15	00	18	32	13	17	32	-15
50.	75	-06	-07	11	-10	10	-02	-01	23	-05
51.	-03	33	13	07	11	34	20	22	14	-02
52.	-01	09	16	11	17	57	17	-11	13	00
53.	-05	09	20	13	15	53	13	-01	37	-02
54.	02	05	16	13	06	57	18	03	-01	-22
55.	11	-03	11	18	10	51	20	-03	02	-07
56.	-11	33	17	15	13	07	-08	03	-05	45
57.	14	08	08	29	01	63	10	10	-04	21
58.	06	12	13	25	04	71	13	14	03	18
59.	01	11	13	21	-03	71	18	17	05	13
60.	17	06	07	25	01	69	14	09	-02	17
61.	10	11	03	21	15	61	07	06	-20	08
62.	10	09	02	31	-02	54	15	10	00	03
63.	-13	32	19	01	70	01	03	05	07	15
64.	-18	33	19	01	76	04	03	10	00	09
65.	-17	37	16	-01	68	06	07	22	00	03
66.	-16	40	16	00	75	01	06	18	-05	03
67.	-16	35	14	00	75	04	02	20	03	04
68.	-09	26	09	03	70	08	04	21	-11	-08
69.	-14	28	14	00	77	07	06	12	-12	-03
70.	-10	27	13	-01	74	06	10	14	-11	-04
71.	-05	28	14	-01	68	12	08	12	-02	10
72.	05	17	-03	00	25	05	07	65	-01	-12
73.	-15	24	09	-04	**	13	00	55	05	00
74.	-08	25	02	-03	35	08	05	65	05	-01
75.	-11	16	18	06	29	08	-08	61	09	-02
76.	-07	32	02	-07	36	04	04	60	-11	-18
77.	-14	29	16	01	57	16	-12	39	08	02
78.	-15	31	19	03	58	09	-08	39	15	04
79.	-09	25	80	06	15	06	00	08	-00	03
80.	-12	25	81	05	11	02	02	07	00	04
81.	-11	24	82	09	14	03	01	07	05	05
82.	-09	22	89	10	12	06	07	-01	04	00
83.	-10	17	83	10	15	08	03	04	05	03
84.	-08	19	88	10	07	08	05	05	04	00

Factors

Item	I	II	III	IV	V	VI	VII	VIII	IX	X
85.	-05	22	84	10	16	09	05	01	-01	01
86.	-05	22	89	04	09	07	07	01	04	-01
87.	07	09	79	06	01	11	10	-05	15	04
88.	-05	04	72	08	06	13	07	-02	14	06
89.	-02	16	79	09	10	08	11	09	06	-01
90.	04	-04	50	03	14	12	00	14	-04	01
91.	74	09	-15	08	-09	-04	-02	09	-10	-19
92.	67	-03	-07	15	-08	04	-01	-01	20	-04
93.	45	31	12	11	04	06	-06	-05	13	-05
94.	80	05	-13	08	-05	-05	-04	05	-03	-20
95.	72	-20	17	11	-06	15	03	-09	08	-07
96.	59	-03	-02	10	-04	15	13	-04	-13	-06
97.	86	-12	-09	10	-07	00	02	-13	05	-11
98.	76	-18	-08	14	-11	-04	08	00	04	-07
99.	82	-22	-06	13	-08	07	08	-14	08	-09
100.	--	--	--	--	--	--	--	--	--	--
101.	82	-21	-05	13	-10	03	07	-11	17	-09
102.	17	-20	13	05	20	26	20	-14	23	29
103.	61	-26	08	11	11	05	06	-03	40	12
104.	73	06	-18	10	-17	03	11	07	-16	-26
105.	65	02	-14	05	-09	08	15	03	28	-20
106.	71	-03	-10	11	-08	11	02	-08	-20	06
107.	58	13	05	13	-15	05	25	-08	-03	18
108.	74	01	00	06	-08	04	14	-04	00	26
109.	72	03	05	04	-05	-01	17	-06	04	28
110.	64	16	01	05	-02	01	26	-09	11	27
111.	66	-17	-05	07	01	08	13	-08	06	40
112.	52	-23	02	13	07	17	09	-18	21	49
113.	78	-11	-04	10	-11	05	13	-10	08	15
114.	46	20	00	03	-06	04	33	13	-06	19
115.	32	-04	02	09	14	15	17	-09	-03	65
116.	34	18	06	09	-04	02	37	00	04	17
117.	27	21	09	15	-10	05	38	-06	08	17
118.	24	-01	06	17	08	20	72	-01	00	00
119.	25	00	09	20	05	21	68	-01	-02	00
120.	21	-04	07	21	08	19	68	01	-01	00
121.	18	-05	08	15	12	17	57	02	-18	04
122.	15	-05	20	43	01	18	42	-10	23	09
123.	15	-03	20	44	-02	17	44	-06	24	09
124.	24	-08	04	44	-03	14	52	-07	00	10
125.	16	-09	04	38	05	20	62	-02	-07	01
126.	22	-03	04	32	-01	20	58	-04	-04	05
127.	44	-12	02	30	-04	01	29	01	02	12
128.	09	08	-13	11	21	15	13	-04	-37	-28
129.	26	06	03	38	-02	21	15	-24	18	-08
130.	08	19	10	26	-02	13	03	-17	22	-09
131.	06	-04	-02	25	-03	15	48	09	-03	-20

Factors

Item	I	II	III	IV	V	VI	VII	VIII	IX	X
132.	14	-01	-07	37	-05	24	25	06	09	-04
133.	09	32	11	31	04	15	26	01	07	-01
134.	01	11	06	56	00	06	23	13	-21	-01
135.	09	32	01	33	05	07	24	-10	25	-15
136.	13	33	-09	41	08	12	21	-08	-05	04
137.	10	12	17	71	00	13	16	-11	04	03
138.	09	07	16	74	-01	12	14	-10	06	06
139.	05	15	18	66	-03	01	06	-05	-05	14
140.	19	-04	05	64	04	01	05	12	01	-03
141.	07	-07	08	67	03	04	10	03	13	09
142.	28	-07	-05	50	-08	-10	15	08	07	04
143.	12	-02	09	44	17	01	11	00	-15	-18
144.	15	-04	09	68	00	12	12	-08	04	04
145.	07	12	10	48	-11	-01	-08	-19	29	02
146.	14	12	00	50	-02	13	06	-17	01	04
147.	00	07	-01	67	00	09	18	15	-15	00
148.	04	08	06	64	-01	27	20	04	-20	-06
149.	11	-02	04	66	00	17	-02	-10	10	17
150.	13	02	-03	62	06	28	-01	00	15	02
151.	10	10	00	59	06	23	00	08	03	-07
152.	09	03	-05	68	04	00	-02	13	-25	02

Eigenvalues

I	II	III	IV	V	VI	VII	VIII	IX	X
14.07	13.91	9.95	9.45	8.44	6.07	5.77	5.64	3.76	3.42

Note: Factor loadings are rounded to two decimal places; decimal points are omitted.

APPENDIX J

Initial Principal Factors Factor Analysis of IMPORTANCE Responses: Orthogonal Transformation Using Varimax Rotation, Retaining Factors With Eigenvalues Greater Than 1

Factors

Item	I	II	III	IV	V	VI	VII	VIII	IX	X
1.	18	-03	65	05	04	06	-04	-11	08	09
2.	17	10	63	04	00	02	-01	03	16	-03
3.	16	06	64	15	09	10	07	02	08	12
4.	07	-02	63	18	10	03	17	19	05	09
5.	10	-13	52	17	18	-02	39	13	06	05
6.	16	03	54	09	12	04	30	17	03	-08
7.	17	-02	60	13	17	04	12	21	02	03
8.	14	-01	60	11	17	03	06	12	-09	01
9.	21	-01	58	10	16	00	03	25	-05	-03
10.	29	08	51	03	-02	-02	-03	15	08	02
11.	24	21	24	04	19	21	09	09	03	11
12.	16	07	54	14	12	07	05	01	10	14
13.	18	07	62	09	12	04	02	21	-04	-03
14.	05	04	48	20	09	03	00	-01	-11	18
15.	18	-06	51	30	03	08	-01	-02	05	24
16.	05	-07	57	35	11	-02	16	16	01	10
17.	05	04	38	17	07	10	12	37	-06	-03
18.	25	44	04	00	02	14	09	10	05	22
19.	03	23	-01	-07	06	14	12	23	01	01
20.	-01	-10	35	24	09	03	17	17	09	06
21.	10	-12	31	32	07	15	28	08	30	-04
22.	28	06	41	20	05	12	04	13	10	27
23.	12	-18	18	33	14	15	29	-05	40	10
24.	05	15	-02	26	08	08	46	06	24	-11
25.	-01	12	28	24	-03	-09	-04	15	-27	-03
26.	13	17	29	42	-09	01	-06	-09	-26	15
27.	-04	-09	21	23	19	00	49	15	-03	-05
28.	08	00	16	27	14	04	63	01	04	03
29.	-04	12	27	20	10	03	45	35	-15	-05
30.	-01	-15	15	35	23	08	68	06	08	03
31.	-01	18	33	30	02	00	25	28	-33	01
32.	03	01	27	39	11	05	44	19	-15	10
33.	-01	-16	15	38	22	03	67	05	08	06
34.	04	02	16	07	04	03	14	45	-02	-12
35.	19	04	20	14	10	11	05	58	03	07
36.	18	12	27	12	13	12	01	59	11	04
37.	18	07	25	20	06	10	-04	67	04	07

Factors

Item	I	II	III	IV	V	VI	VII	VIII	IX	X
38.	08	00	26	29	11	17	07	39	-01	19
39.	23	24	12	-06	02	28	19	25	06	12
40.	08	13	19	19	13	31	25	32	00	01
41.	28	04	66	13	03	13	02	-08	-08	-04
42.	22	04	62	15	04	13	03	-12	-05	-08
43.	18	15	54	10	08	08	13	15	-05	-18
44.	16	08	57	15	15	01	-03	31	-09	-10
45.	13	06	52	18	12	07	02	18	-10	-13
46.	13	-08	35	37	12	13	17	17	-21	06
47.	05	13	30	18	12	11	16	36	-12	-15
48.	08	15	32	12	11	12	20	31	-06	-19
49.	12	14	16	18	13	42	24	33	-05	-04
50.	11	75	-01	-10	-12	20	06	08	-13	-09
51.	15	11	24	24	12	41	11	30	-07	11
52.	34	13	10	07	15	49	10	21	-09	13
53.	30	02	06	12	20	52	17	22	19	00
54.	36	12	07	18	13	49	02	12	-07	11
55.	41	21	05	12	14	42	14	05	02	11
56.	41	07	29	06	14	23	14	10	25	-10
57.	52	20	13	08	10	56	-06	01	03	-01
58.	47	18	10	14	14	63	-03	11	04	-05
59.	46	17	10	16	14	61	-05	12	04	-03
60.	50	20	11	11	11	61	-05	04	04	-01
61.	44	13	22	25	02	41	-01	-08	-04	01
62.	53	17	19	13	07	49	-06	07	02	01
63.	18	-10	37	57	23	15	10	01	26	-14
64.	11	-11	30	67	22	14	14	03	21	-13
65.	06	-14	25	70	22	12	10	07	15	-09
66.	11	-11	32	73	22	08	06	00	16	-11
67.	04	-14	19	74	19	09	15	06	13	-10
68.	19	00	22	67	17	24	-04	11	07	03
69.	21	-01	22	70	19	23	-03	15	15	05
70.	22	00	20	68	19	25	-03	16	17	05
71.	16	03	18	65	19	19	-03	19	18	-01
72.	16	-08	16	65	07	01	11	02	-24	12
73.	04	-13	09	69	10	-06	25	03	-17	09
74.	05	-09	10	73	10	-04	21	07	-17	11
75.	01	-03	10	62	13	02	38	08	-16	06
76.	08	-05	22	73	09	-04	01	01	-33	18
77.	04	-13	11	68	19	-03	34	16	-01	-07
78.	04	-12	12	65	23	-02	35	17	01	-11
79.	13	-06	23	25	71	05	08	05	-03	-04
80.	16	-08	28	26	68	08	07	11	-02	-01
81.	11	-08	20	22	81	03	15	03	02	-03
82.	16	-05	23	17	85	06	04	07	01	-02
83.	02	-04	11	15	83	07	21	-01	00	-04

Factors

Item	I	II	III	IV	V	VI	VII	VIII	IX	X
84.	06	-07	14	16	87	04	14	02	-02	-02
85.	15	-02	26	22	79	04	06	-01	01	00
86.	26	-05	24	17	77	02	-02	14	01	01
87.	14	06	-02	04	73	10	01	12	12	06
88.	14	04	-01	12	70	07	02	16	06	06
89.	21	03	11	14	73	11	12	06	00	05
90.	14	11	-02	14	41	16	09	-02	-03	11
91.	11	82	08	-05	-09	06	-07	00	-23	-06
92.	15	76	-03	-13	-04	10	= =02	03	-05	-16
93.	09	54	17	01	13	-03	05	18	-04	-23
94.	13	81	08	-02	-08	04	-05	-02	-23	-07
95.	24	76	-07	-10	09	19	07	03	-10	01
96.	27	63	05	-01	-01	19	-05	-04	-13	11
97.	19	86	-03	-12	-10	06	-02	-01	-15	-08
98.	17	78	-11	-11	-04	11	07	00	-07	01
99.	23	82	-11	-17	-05	08	00	00	-10	-02
100.	--	--	--	--	--	--	--	--	--	--
101.	22	81	-09	-15	-04	09	03	02	-09	-07
102.	31	26	01	14	15	28	18	-11	27	09
103.	21	65	-15	09	06	14	23	-03	10	-09
104.	18	69	14	09	-12	02	-21	-07	-28	07
105.	25	62	15	15	12	06	-19	-16	-23	13
106.	28	71	11	04	-09	07	03	-16	00	02
107.	33	63	13	-01	05	-02	-14	16	13	11
108.	23	74	06	00	03	-08	-10	11	23	08
109.	12	72	10	-01	07	-12	-09	07	23	00
110.	22	68	12	-01	08	-07	-11	12	25	14
111.	16	76	-01	-08	-03	02	01	03	35	07
112.	24	63	-03	-08	01	11	08	03	48	03
113.	17	78	00	-09	02	01	-06	10	17	09
114.	16	56	16	09	06	-02	-02	20	16	22
115.	16	51	11	07	02	05	08	04	48	13
116.	30	46	20	03	08	02	-07	20	12	20
117.	38	35	26	04	07	00	-07	16	06	13
118.	60	27	17	07	12	14	-01	03	00	45
119.	62	27	19	06	12	13	-03	02	04	44
120.	64	26	14	08	09	18	01	-03	01	43
121.	55	25	16	17	10	13	03	-05	06	49
122.	71	21	10	01	18	11	00	07	06	09
123.	74	20	10	02	17	11	00	09	06	09
124.	67	25	11	-03	07	15	-07	00	03	18
125.	70	17	12	07	09	12	-06	02	-06	25
126.	64	30	13	-03	07	10	-05	02	-03	25
127.	51	47	00	-02	11	10	07	01	00	16
128.	33	08	24	22	01	01	01	-08	13	03

Factors

Item	I	II	III	IV	V	VI	VII	VIII	IX	X
129.	68	18	23	03	05	07	-08	20	02	-04
130.	58	11	26	07	02	-07	-13	30	-03	-05
131.	60	13	11	13	06	12	-07	06	-11	21
132.	64	15	09	04	05	18	00	08	-06	14
133.	50	08	39	13	07	-03	-10	09	-09	-05
134.	70	12	18	11	06	12	02	-04	-02	09
135.	56	09	27	12	02	-10	-18	29	-12	-10
136.	54	13	43	11	05	-06	-11	03	-03	-10
137.	77	16	11	-02	14	04	01	18	02	-07
138.	75	16	12	01	15	07	04	14	03	-10
139.	73	08	09	05	16	02	06	10	12	-09
140.	66	22	11	08	10	09	17	-08	-03	04
141.	69	12	05	-01	10	18	16	04	12	-07
142.	59	35	-06	04	02	10	10	-04	05	08
143.	55	17	09	13	06	15	12	-16	-02	20
144.	76	20	09	02	06	11	06	-04	08	03
145.	58	09	08	04	12	-06	00	18	06	-25
146.	64	09	16	10	05	-04	-07	11	03	-17
147.	68	13	19	11	09	01	02	02	-03	03
148.	74	12	17	11	05	09	02	01	-05	05
149.	57	14	09	00	00	03	14	11	11	-20
150.	67	15	08	10	03	16	05	11	06	-18
151.	61	13	10	11	04	13	11	06	-01	-10
152.	66	10	18	09	-02	12	05	-11	-04	-03
	4.80	4.39	4.29	2.90	2.54					

Eigenvalues

I	II	III	IV	V	VI	VII	VIII	IX	X
19.35	15.25	11.31	10.81	8.53	4.80	4.39	4.29	2.90	2.54

Note: Factor loadings are rounded to two decimal places; decimal points are omitted.

APPENDIX K

Initial Principal Factor Factor Analysis of FREQUENCY Responses: Oblique Transformation Using Promax Rotation, Retaining Factors With Eigenvalues Greater Than 1

Factors

Item	I	II	III	IV	V	VI	VII	VIII	IX	X
1.	-14	56	18	09	19	19	05	02	-12	03
2.	02	46	10	16	06	17	03	06	05	28
3.	-15	69	22	12	36	29	06	09	-12	04
4.	-23	73	27	06	51	30	05	09	00	01
5.	-28	63	33	06	49	38	-03	11	01	01
6.	-14	64	30	09	41	35	-04	09	20	06
7.	-18	61	28	02	37	30	01	08	03	02
8.	-09	60	24	07	41	27	20	16	06	-11
9.	-04	53	23	01	30	17	08	11	27	-01
10.	-08	42	14	05	07	14	-13	-05	04	14
11.	20	20	22	19	07	24	21	24	21	15
12.	-07	52	20	10	26	20	13	10	-03	16
13.	-07	58	27	06	23	27	02	05	21	12
14.	-07	55	13	10	35	17	08	13	-14	-07
15.	-37	62	17	07	-52	30	-04	-10	-32	-04
16.	-30	69	24	03	-54	33	01	00	-15	-04
17.	-13	53	28	07	45	27	04	10	21	-01
18.	46	-05	-07	23	-03	-11	24	05	02	13
19.	33	-15	03	09	-11	-08	00	08	39	13
20.	-33	52	30	06	-41	30	-08	-02	03	11
21.	-26	37	26	09	27	61	-04	15	16	29
22.	-06	35	25	13	17	30	42	24	11	07
23.	-31	10	28	02	04	57	01	22	28	41
24.	13	-11	21	05	-01	44	-07	11	44	26
25.	06	55	-01	04	-51	-06	-02	-11	-13	-25
26.	17	42	-07	03	-44	-03	13	-01	-28	-15
27.	-11	33	23	11	43	25	-09	17	21	20
28.	-18	26	29	12	42	29	-12	13	12	18
29.	-09	48	27	04	50	14	-07	07	31	03
30.	-30	35	35	08	54	38	-12	12	12	21
31.	10	51	06	03	56	-01	01	09	-04	-16
32.	-14	43	26	-05	57	22	00	13	05	03
33.	-38	38	34	06	60	39	-15	06	07	17
34.	-03	21	15	04	13	06	-02	06	34	02
35.	-19	29	29	02	30	21	07	09	35	07
36.	-02	31	14	06	18	16	09	16	31	23
37.	-13	39	16	00	33	15	04	04	29	11

Factors

Item	I	II	III	IV	V	VI	VII	VIII	IX	X
130.	10	10	15	29	-02	00	16	15	31	09
131.	16	00	03	30	02	-03	51	28	-06	-09
132.	22	-04	-01	41	00	-04	37	34	12	08
133.	11	30	22	38	12	12	35	30	17	10
134.	08	20	14	57	13	03	35	26	-14	05
135.	13	25	12	37	05	09	32	20	28	02
136.	17	32	04	45	06	09	33	27	04	16
137.	16	12	23	77	-04	04	37	30	24	18
138.	16	06	22	79	-08	04	35	30	23	20
139.	09	16	24	67	00	03	23	19	12	23
140.	26	00	09	63	03	02	23	22	04	06
141.	15	-06	15	66	-08	10	23	28	15	15
142.	36	-08	-03	49	-12	-08	25	13	04	08
143.	14	07	09	44	09	07	27	12	-05	-04
144.	23	-03	13	71	-11	01	32	30	16	17
145.	11	01	15	46	-16	-04	05	10	35	15
146.	19	09	05	52	-09	-03	23	23	14	17
147.	10	16	09	67	09	04	31	33	-13	03
148.	13	17	14	68	07	02	39	44	-07	03
149.	18	-04	11	67	-13	04	18	32	22	27
150.	20	00	07	65	-01	08	21	43	22	15
151.	16	12	09	60	11	07	21	37	10	04
152.	16	14	01	65	09	01	15	21	-21	04

Eigenvalues

I	II	III	IV	V	VI	VII	VIII	IX	X
16.32	16.40	13.98	12.49	14.06	12.98	10.56	10.30	6.01	4.80

Note: Factor loadings are rounded to two decimal places; decimal points are omitted.

APPENDIX L

Initial Principal Factors Factor Analysis of IMPORTANCE Responses: Oblique Transformation Using Promax Rotation, Retaining Factors With Eigenvalues Greater Than 1

Factors

Item	I	II	III	IV	V	VI	VII	VIII	IX	X
1.	27	02	65	25	16	15	-03	09	11	18
2.	30	14	64	23	13	13	-02	22	18	07
3.	29	10	69	36	25	22	10	24	12	22
4.	20	00	68	40	27	14	23	38	10	12
5.	20	-11	59	39	35	11	43	31	12	06
6.	29	07	61	31	29	19	33	36	10	-02
7.	31	03	37	36	34	18	17	40	10	09
8.	26	03	65	33	31	15	12	31	-02	07
9.	34	05	65	33	32	15	08	43	02	04
10.	39	15	56	21	12	11	-06	31	13	12
11.	35	26	34	18	28	35	10	23	11	23
12.	28	11	59	32	26	20	08	21	14	23
13.	33	13	68	31	27	18	06	40	03	06
14.	15	06	51	34	20	12	06	15	-08	24
15.	26	-02	58	46	19	20	04	16	09	32
16.	17	-06	65	54	29	11	25	35	05	14
17.	18	06	46	32	21	19	19	47	-01	00
18.	34	49	13	04	07	29	04	18	09	34
19.	10	24	03	-03	08	18	12	25	04	04
20.	07	-11	40	37	22	10	24	29	13	05
21.	18	-12	42	46	24	25	32	22	34	00
22.	38	12	51	37	21	28	06	30	16	37
23.	16	-19	29	45	29	24	33	10	45	12
24.	12	12	09	29	18	21	47	15	28	-07
25.	07	13	32	28	04	-01	03	22	-26	02
26.	20	20	38	43	02	14	01	02	-26	27
27.	03	-11	29	35	31	10	56	25	02	-08
28.	14	-01	26	38	27	20	67	13	10	05
29.	08	11	35	31	23	14	52	44	-10	-05
30.	05	-19	27	47	38	21	76	18	15	00
31.	12	19	41	38	16	13	34	37	-30	05
32.	12	01	39	50	27	20	54	31	-10	11
33.	03	-20	27	49	37	16	75	17	14	02
34.	12	04	23	16	14	09	18	48	02	-12
35.	29	09	33	28	24	23	10	65	11	10
36.	31	17	40	28	28	24	06	69	19	09
37.	30	13	39	34	23	22	02	74	11	11
38.	18	03	38	41	26	26	16	49	06	22

Factors

Item	I	II	III	IV	V	VI	VII	VIII	IX	X
39.	32	31	20	04	11	39	16	32	13	20
40.	21	16	31	31	26	41	32	41	08	07
41.	40	12	71	34	19	28	05	12	-02	10
42.	34	10	66	34	18	26	06	08	-01	06
43.	33	20	61	29	23	23	16	32	01	-07
44.	32	13	65	36	30	15	04	48	-02	-01
45.	27	10	60	36	27	19	09	35	-04	-04
46.	21	-04	47	51	28	26	28	29	-13	11
47.	19	16	40	31	25	22	23	46	-06	-09
48.	22	18	40	26	23	24	25	41	00	-12
49.	25	19	30	31	27	52	32	41	04	04
50.	26	78	02	-14	-13	32	00	11	-13	08
51.	28	16	38	37	27	52	20	40	02	20
52.	43	22	25	22	28	62	13	31	20	26
53.	39	10	23	27	34	64	21	31	31	11
54.	44	22	24	29	25	63	07	21	04	26
55.	50	31	22	23	26	60	15	16	12	28
56.	51	15	42	25	30	41	11	26	35	04
57.	62	34	30	22	23	74	-05	13	15	22
58.	58	31	29	28	28	79	01	22	17	16
59.	57	29	29	29	28	77	-01	23	17	18
60.	60	34	29	24	24	78	-03	15	16	22
61.	52	24	38	36	17	59	02	05	05	22
62.	62	31	37	28	22	67	-05	20	13	23
63.	30	-11	55	73	43	31	21	22	34	-03
64.	22	-13	49	79	42	30	28	22	28	-04
65.	16	-16	44	80	41	26	27	23	22	-02
66.	22	-13	51	83	41	24	21	19	22	-01
67.	13	-18	38	81	38	22	31	21	19	-05
68.	31	02	43	76	36	41	12	27	15	16
69.	33	01	45	80	40	41	12	33	23	17
70.	34	02	44	78	39	43	11	33	25	18
71.	29	04	39	73	38	35	11	34	25	11
72.	24	09	34	67	23	21	24	14	-19	22
73.	07	-16	25	70	25	08	40	12	-14	11
74.	10	-11	28	74	26	12	37	16	-13	14
75.	08	-06	27	66	29	18	52	18	-11	09
76.	14	-05	38	75	25	12	19	13	-29	25
77.	11	-16	31	74	37	14	49	28	05	-05
78.	11	-16	31	72	40	14	50	29	07	-09
79.	25	-06	39	45	79	22	22	25	12	02
80.	29	-07	44	48	78	26	22	31	13	05
81.	23	-09	36	43	87	20	29	23	17	02
82.	29	-05	39	40	91	24	18	28	18	05
83.	13	-08	24	34	86	20	35	17	15	-01
84.	18	-09	28	36	90	19	29	21	14	01

Factors

Item	I	II	III	IV	V	VI	VII	VIII	IX	X
85.	28	-03	41	44	86	22	20	22	16	08
86.	38	-02	41	41	85	22	11	34	18	09
87.	24	06	12	19	74	24	09	26	27	11
88.	24	04	14	26	72	21	13	29	21	11
89.	32	05	27	33	79	29	24	24	16	13
90.	21	12	10	22	44	28	16	08	06	18
91.	27	85	11	-09	-10	21	-12	07	-24	14
92.	30	78	01	-17	-06	24	-06	08	-04	02
93.	26	55	23	06	17	12	04	29	-01	-10
94.	29	84	11	-07	-09	20	-10	05	-23	13
95.	38	80	01	-11	08	38	01	10	-05	21
96.	39	69	13	00	01	36	-10	04	-10	32
97.	33	89	00	-18	-13	22	-11	04	-15	13
98.	30	81	-06	-17	-07	26	-02	04	-06	18
99.	35	87	-06	-23	-09	25	-10	04	-09	17
100.	--	--	--	--	--	--	--	--	--	--
101.	36	85	-04	-20	-06	26	-06	07	-07	13
102.	39	30	14	21	24	45	16	02	34	24
103.	33	66	-03	05	08	33	17	05	13	08
104.	31	73	18	05	-11	18	-24	01	-29	27
105.	36	67	21	11	-09	23	-22	-06	-23	35
106.	41	75	18	03	-05	27	-05	-03	01	25
107.	47	68	22	04	10	19	-22	29	17	30
108.	38	75	13	00	15	12	-19	24	24	26
109.	29	71	14	-01	07	05	-17	20	23	16
110.	37	70	18	02	10	12	-18	26	27	30
111.	30	76	03	-10	-03	18	-11	13	35	23
112.	36	64	04	-06	04	26	-05	15	50	19
113.	32	79	05	-10	01	17	-16	20	18	26
114.	31	57	24	14	12	16	-05	33	19	35
115.	29	50	18	11	08	20	00	19	49	26
116.	43	51	30	12	16	21	-11	34	17	35
117.	49	42	36	15	17	20	-11	31	12	28
118.	66	41	33	20	24	41	-06	19	10	64
119.	68	40	35	21	25	39	-07	19	14	64
120.	69	40	31	21	21	44	-04	12	12	63
121.	60	36	32	28	23	38	00	12	15	67
122.	77	36	29	17	31	39	-06	22	19	30
123.	79	35	29	17	30	40	-06	23	19	30
124.	72	40	26	09	18	40	-14	13	13	40
125.	73	33	30	20	22	39	-10	15	05	45
126.	69	45	27	09	17	35	-12	16	07	46
127.	59	57	14	04	17	35	00	12	08	36
128.	38	13	34	31	13	18	00	06	16	16
129.	75	34	40	19	20	33	-14	33	13	16

	Factors				
Item	I	II	III	IV	V
40.	4101	0432	0402	2274	1941
41.	5072	-0009	1283	0500	0758
42.	4844	-0503	1569	-0304	0918
43.	5071	1120	0845	1568	-0096
44.	6770	0043	0478	1245	0296
45.	5988	0952	0791	0659	0208
46.	5370	-1190	-0008	0739	2811
47.	5053	0939	0376	2496	1131
48.	5287	1140	0611	1640	0710
49.	2559	0961	1480	2141	2726
50.	-0779	7533	1213	-0100	-0919
51.	3294	0096	2509	1579	2621
52.	0461	0312	3705	2253	2705
53.	0385	0131	3318	3351	2894
54.	0733	0306	3871	1336	1672
55.	-0284	1220	4091	1147	1936
56.	2947	-0877	1281	2147	1743
57.	0494	1574	5237	1193	2406
58.	0903	0918	5233	1817	3107
59.	0699	0549	5118	1838	2840
60.	0229	1895	5256	1057	2588
61.	1293	0827	4391	-0039	2820
62.	0667	1174	5087	0586	1571
63.	3936	-1187	0196	2221	5899
64.	4382	-1887	0259	1815	6409
65.	4942	-1714	0321	1308	6106
66.	5325	-1767	0142	1095	6341
67.	4819	-1689	0117	1210	6504
68.	4172	-1272	0546	0147	5846
69.	4268	-1720	0475	0584	6322
70.	4078	-1277	0504	0552	6217
71.	3808	-0515	0643	1174	6112
72.	3578	0250	0194	-1278	3731
73.	4108	-1571	-0146	0190	4447
74.	4309	-0806	-0045	-0557	4902
75.	3605	-1240	0074	1163	3884
76.	5279	-1054	-0537	-1195	4170
77.	4680	-1544	-0139	1177	5662
78.	4729	-1565	-0063	1813	5739
79.	3401	-1035	0756	7348	1242
80.	3158	-1185	0658	7541	0905
81.	3121	-1123	0895	7772	1153
82.	2778	-0963	1396	8416	0748
83.	2437	-0989	1263	7885	1309
84.	2625	-0840	1313	8276	0551
85.	2897	-0322	1425	7820	1184

Item	Factors I	II	III	IV	V
86.	2887	-0507	0985	8348	0636
87.	1021	0885	1416	7749	0394
88.	0735	-0303	1422	7077	0905
89.	2321	-0210	1542	7280	1128
90.	0668	0198	0745	4053	1703
91.	1356	6936	0567	-2244	-1535
92.	-0483	6682	1324	-0228	-1018
93.	2895	4289	1043	1362	-0520
94.	1030	7492	0366	-1971	-1483
95.	-1758	6949	1711	1405	-0728
96.	-0334	5533	2134	-0676	-0336
97.	-1160	8286	0988	-1118	-1612
98.	-1611	7395	1370	-1137	-1435
99.	-2177	8098	1759	-0752	-1305
100.	----	----	----	----	----
101.	-2223	8217	1558	-0273	-1390
102.	-2756	2357	2215	2599	3256
103.	-2706	6465	1125	1875	1413
104.	1011	6843	1534	-2933	-2110
105.	0598	5948	1598	-2809	-1170
106.	-0343	6657	1754	-1646	-0966
107.	0639	5951	2592	0388	-0917
108.	-0281	7549	1470	-0056	-0191
109.	-0170	7381	1281	0629	0064
110.	1012	6477	1939	-0219	0162
111.	-2319	6880	1661	0101	1227
112.	-3355	5676	2160	1549	1896
113.	-1533	7877	1783	-0178	-0760
114.	1684	4761	1980	-0377	0748
115.	-1271	3608	2281	0976	2902
116.	1162	3735	2534	0565	0396
117.	1068	3209	3162	1169	-0187
118.	-0689	2874	5268	0205	2226
119.	-0414	2882	5457	0453	1872
120.	-0708	2472	5311	0229	2081
121.	-0436	1926	4295	-0040	2241
122.	-1085	1939	5977	2619	0599
123.	-0880	1945	6073	2635	0443
124.	-1278	2577	6409	0290	0292
125.	-1088	1805	6483	-0046	1296
126.	-0786	2412	5891	0154	0922
127.	-1258	4425	3731	0090	-0042
128.	0864	0591	2255	-1821	2212
129.	-0070	2675	4473	0941	-1004
130.	1346	0957	2674	1683	-1059
131.	-0351	0724	4477	-0659	0497

Factors

Item	I	II	III	IV	V
132.	-0298	1521	4773	-0424	0234
133.	2831	1073	4167	1197	0365
134.	1726	-0328	5745	-0280	-0351
135.	2615	1184	3852	0770	-0385
136.	2795	1294	4721	-0644	0099
137.	1248	0659	7118	1668	-1367
138.	0725	0574	7161	1703	-1370
139.	1643	0126	5756	1553	-1488
140.	0488	1364	5320	0058	-0684
141.	-0399	0443	5864	1121	-0340
142.	-0498	2621	4159	-0466	-1240
143.	0887	0496	3998	-0216	-0021
144.	-0184	1171	6492	0883	-1006
145.	0584	0740	3407	2043	-2374
146.	0839	1251	4804	0273	-1246
147.	1298	-0508	6524	-0770	-0400
148.	1317	-0088	7103	-0221	-0431
149.	-0292	0931	5855	1077	-0702
150.	0317	1096	5974	0342	0110
151.	1533	0600	5509	-0053	-0067
152.	1372	0031	5508	-1515	-0886

Eigenvalues

Item	I	II	III	IV	V
	16.34	13.86	13.63	9.57	8.52

Note: Factor loadings are rounded to four decimal places; decimal points are omitted.

APPENDIX N

Five Factor Solution for a Factor Analysis of IMPORTANCE Responses: Orthogonal Transformation Using Varimax Rotation

Factors

Item	I	II	III	IV	V
1.	2360	-0712	0532	5432	-0125
2.	1915	0738	0370	5743	-0027
3.	2141	0459	2012	5734	0515
4.	0806	-0137	2621	6287	0995
5.	0733	-1093	3258	5109	2105
6.	1320	0466	2248	5517	1600
7.	1796	-0131	1911	6177	1685
8.	1429	-0222	1480	6054	1267
9.	1924	-0070	1217	6385	1435
10.	2866	0638	0035	5296	-0181
11.	3020	2270	1289	2239	1870
12.	2140	0546	1755	4782	0867
13.	1848	0698	1113	6529	0971
14.	1007	0112	2042	4475	-0025
15.	2556	-0868	2954	4473	-0452
16.	0611	-0742	3993	5815	0684
17.	0502	0724	2430	4712	0919
18.	2992	4563	0584	0482	0242
19.	0377	2722	0282	0501	1213
20.	0006	-0868	3115	3580	1046
21.	1376	-1013	4356	2615	1230
22.	3508	0572	2404	3940	0196
23.	1849	-1670	4589	0806	1920
24.	0368	1835	4268	-0374	1730
25.	-0140	1054	1798	3657	-1180
26.	1624	1214	3383	2757	-2456
27.	-0889	-0472	4212	2375	2320
28.	0476	0405	5129	1183	1834
29.	-0993	1757	3811	3668	1458
30.	-0284	-1012	6249	1160	2927
31.	-0449	2024	3784	4288	0223
32.	0129	0439	5545	3066	0962
33.	-0422	-1156	6329	1192	2683
34.	-0106	0770	1380	3026	1150
35.	1871	0968	1851	3721	1597
36.	1883	1734	1588	4365	2039
37.	1792	1318	2013	4523	1158
38.	1336	0383	3500	3445	1111

Factors

Item	I	II	III	IV	V
39.	2741	2993	0844	1396	0988
40.	1297	1957	3498	2378	1859
41.	3208	0021	1463	5789	-0370
42.	2584	0041	1635	5291	-0267
43.	1679	1477	1534	5563	0877
44.	1470	0760	1413	6566	1208
45.	1276	0592	1935	5655	0896
46.	1468	-0674	4435	3830	0615
47.	0323	1717	2566	4106	1472
48.	0539	1907	2161	3997	1484
49.	1864	2100	3593	2051	1862
50.	1330	7649	-0507	0087	-1105
51.	2491	1571	3663	2706	1228
52.	4584	1813	2194	0889	1994
53.	4134	0872	2952	0420	2950
54.	4801	1549	2709	0569	1166
55.	5107	2405	2420	0165	1523
56.	4514	0815	1471	2608	2095
57.	6574	2178	1504	0635	0995
58.	6126	2183	2322	0615	1573
59.	6072	2028	2351	0669	1532
60.	6476	2276	1921	0477	1142
61.	5497	1195	2802	1469	-0293
62.	6438	1828	1779	1543	0584
63.	2346	-1243	5839	3213	2038
64.	1581	-1241	6866	2696	1856
65.	1091	-1474	7009	2446	1706
66.	1560	-1385	6880	2995	1382
67.	0748	-1541	7442	1942	1408
68.	2880	-0093	6427	2242	0871
69.	3069	-0178	6705	2396	1264
70.	3243	-0055	6503	2196	1268
71.	2420	0311	6080	2131	1445
72.	1799	0521	6175	1981	-0728
73.	0202	-1440	7049	1278	-0066
74.	0437	-0970	7301	1485	-0102
75.	0038	-0174	7180	1367	0690
76.	0999	-0876	6528	2614	-0977
77.	0115	-1160	7396	1775	1605
78.	0017	-0173	7220	1806	2074
79.	1522	-0644	3006	2585	6469
80.	1899	-0789	3153	3116	6244
81.	1278	-0847	3030	2155	7551
82.	1904	-0595	2224	2595	7856
83.	0420	-0374	2753	1098	7944
84.	0800	-0657	2553	1565	8166

Item	Factors I	II	III	IV	V
85.	1810	-0401	2662	2590	7129
86.	2803	-0619	1837	2985	-7128
87.	1893	0780	0975	0246	-7239
88.	1719	0508	1663	0545	-6765
89.	2448	0366	2285	1326	6915
90.	1955	1164	2121	-0285	-3716
91.	1204	8055	-0875	1092	-1499
92.	1514	7603	-1263	-0064	-0283
93.	0436	5466	0086	2552	1402
94.	1321	7921	-0646	1051	-1467
95.	2726	7688	-0466	-0582	0861
96.	3275	6141	-0092	0366	-0724
97.	1829	8471	-1430	-0046	-1266
98.	1882	7866	-0751	-1011	-0456
99.	2310	8251	-1678	-0842	-0585
100.	----	----	----	----	----
101.	2226	8170	-1384	-0605	-0346
102.	4014	2654	2479	-0913	1812
103.	2176	6638	1646	-1587	0878
104.	2104	6445	-0283	1541	-2575
105.	3040	5654	0341	1205	-2689
106.	3054	6808	0263	0568	-1374
107.	3516	6097	-0921	1912	0317
108.	2425	7220	-0766	1061	0313
109.	1237	6987	-0866	1317	0619
110.	2423	6665	-0753	1519	0748
111.	1974	7581	-0837	-0314	0211
112.	2853	6424	-0392	-0701	1026
113.	1972	7791	-1171	0300	0351
114.	1971	5572	0737	2049	0513
115.	2201	5070	0988	0655	0760
116.	3353	4556	0045	2549	0630
117.	3898	3362	-0028	3094	0437
118.	6809	2621	0804	1600	0527
119.	6935	2519	0680	1727	0632
120.	7223	2454	1052	1012	0251
121.	6367	2294	1880	1075	0259
122.	7254	2034	0034	1330	1735
123.	7502	1902	0070	1318	1609
124.	7173	2350	-0520	1017	0442
125.	7386	1562	0368	1300	0327
126.	6777	2868	-0458	1355	0265
127.	5325	4692	0051	0049	0873
128.	3463	0472	1835	2014	-0319
129.	6630	1741	-0315	3112	0452

Factors

Item	I	II	III	IV	V
130.	5279	0991	-0397	3937	0109
131.	6317	1143	0876	1405	-0056
132.	6682	1486	0457	1132	0286
133.	4788	0489	0482	4434	0105
134.	7192	0968	1016	1648	0188
135.	4915	0715	-0185	4215	-0182
136.	5067	0852	0114	4562	-0134
137.	7224	1517	-0498	1980	1524
138.	7116	1611	-0063	1843	1693
139.	6842	0743	0351	1406	1837
140.	6511	2110	1121	0875	0778
141.	6844	1280	0558	0536	1538
142.	5996	3480	0549	-0661	0190
143.	5911	1467	1736	0283	0086
144.	7574	1889	0167	0807	0572
145.	5036	0899	-0214	1895	1469
146.	5861	0658	0060	2383	0384
147.	6607	1017	0711	2201	0528
148.	7322	1012	0804	1876	0130
149.	5154	1444	0154	1338	0667
150.	6545	1488	0879	1254	0575
151.	5874	1317	1280	1325	0511
152.	6592	0770	0833	1439	-0518

Eigenvalues

Item	I	II	III	IV	V
	21.85	15.16	13.71	12.56	8.02

Note: Factor loadings are rounded to four decimal places; decimal points are omitted.

APPENDIX O

Five-Factor Solution for a Factor Analysis of FREQUENCY Responses: Oblique Transformation Using Promax Rotation

	Factors				
Item	I	II	III	IV	V
1.	4963	-1434	0902	1124	1467
2.	3876	0513	1458	1089	1222
3.	6425	-1617	1266	1417	2839
4.	7288	-2202	0711	1976	3457
5.	6447	2773	0460	2610	3944
6.	6656	-1273	0634	2809	3244
7.	5934	-1752	0361	2267	2978
8.	5950	-0884	1475	1821	3112
9.	5470	-0160	0648	2381	1872
10.	3820	-0746	-0134	1310	0604
11.	1893	2369	2614	2429	2316
12.	4664	-0463	1437	1517	2408
13.	5660	-0329	0657	2724	2224
14.	5223	-0953	1204	0516	2016
15.	5929	-4022	-0972	0311	3455
16.	6802	-3185	-0291	1270	3722
17.	5808	-1102	0751	2542	3012
18.	-0462	4623	2480	-0662	-0755
19.	-0887	3657	0868	1207	-0886
20.	5330	-3076	-0792	2432	3331
21.	3610	-1976	0752	2834	5560
22.	2924	-0030	2971	2404	3524
23.	0701	-1968	0716	3596	5430
24.	-0515	1719	0226	3163	3498
25.	6025	-0127	-0727	-1189	0146
26.	4286	1111	0114	-1932	1025
27.	4090	-0723	0770	2364	3379
28.	3353	-1529	0533	2642	3565
29.	5857	-0737	0095	2597	2190
30.	4345	-2569	0208	3130	4747
31.	5757	0540	0326	-0311	1254
32.	4859	-1268	-0165	1932	3682
33.	4721	-3480	-0187	2859	4781
34.	2680	0047	0414	2008	0512
35.	3503	-1297	0597	3178	2586
36.	3205	0473	1171	1947	2166
37.	4408	0840	0260	1820	2161
38.	4293	-1933	0685	2035	3511

Factors

Item	I	II	III	IV	V
39.	1451	1820	2012	2209	1046
40.	4179	-0171	0902	3096	3246
41.	5105	-0403	1549	1537	2194
42.	4914	-0780	1669	0802	2224
43.	4983	0615	1381	2369	1419
44.	6804	-0718	0896	2343	2251
45.	5897	0347	1273	1660	1798
46.	5585	-1975	0172	1895	4260
47.	5050	0243	1004	3341	2708
48.	5226	0512	1195	2528	2225
49.	2637	0701	1993	2972	3607
50.	-1529	7699	2434	-0390	-1742
51.	3447	0010	2833	2711	3771
52.	0649	0768	3973	3120	3320
53.	0624	0474	3657	4142	3652
54.	0856	0856	4040	2178	2274
55.	-0235	1897	4361	1874	2159
56.	3161	-1111	1466	2954	2949
57.	0541	2353	5598	2253	2865
58.	1055	1606	5571	3023	3801
59.	0877	1263	5379	2976	3529
60.	0249	2693	5655	2095	2916
61.	1377	1381	4584	1124	3257
62.	0699	1984	5314	1585	2047
63.	4325	-1994	0523	3501	7076
64.	4847	-2728	0463	3267	7678
65.	5361	-2578	0529	2829	7436
66.	5749	-2717	0350	2683	7710
67.	5247	-2601	0331	2730	7745
68.	4514	-1959	0686	1576	6772
69.	4683	-2461	0593	2075	7360
70.	4447	-1997	0685	1993	7165
71.	4119	-1213	0990	2537	7037
72.	3648	-0313	0398	-0244	4204
73.	4415	-2301	-0084	1352	5418
74.	4540	-1563	0108	0701	5704
75.	3891	-1877	0231	2176	4908
76.	5475	-1954	-0448	0079	5136
77.	5057	-2446	0071	2536	6874
78.	5130	-2482	0201	3181	7075
79.	3742	-1572	1366	7931	3442
80.	3506	-1696	1239	8032	3103
81.	3483	-1605	1508	8314	3379
82.	3135	-1306	2053	8909	3044
83.	2805	-1333	1874	8388	3388
84.	2959	-1170	1968	8711	2776
85.	3222	-0989	2108	8393	3352

Factors

Item	I	II	III	IV	V
86.	3187	-0952	1726	8769	2874
87.	1178	0739	2250	7897	1966
88.	1010	-0386	1993	7301	2382
89.	2594	-0477	2222	7779	3030
90.	0834	0027	1185	4333	2502
91.	0559	6848	1595	-2294	-2135
92.	-1158	6873	2394	-0435	-1687
93.	2492	4015	2001	1714	0128
94.	0187	7372	1505	-2122	-2195
95.	-2390	7288	2908	1038	-1457
96.	-0872	5881	2975	-0606	-0900
97.	-2040	8505	2222	-1574	-2758
98.	-2390	7761	2424	-1553	-2589
99.	-2999	8568	2938	-1215	-2585
100.	----	----	----	----	----
101.	-3050	8636	2798	-0802	-2624
102.	-2737	2780	2771	2735	2754
103.	-3196	6668	2308	1524	0403
104.	0196	7053	2436	-2930	-2794
105.	-0085	6487	2362	-2724	-1895
106.	-1047	6965	2700	-1716	-1804
107.	0067	6264	3613	0561	-1026
108.	-1002	7665	2736	-0149	-0902
109.	-0849	7412	2591	0538	-0516
110.	0404	6555	3063	0037	-0122
111.	-2900	7206	2769	-0091	0028
112.	-3739	6173	3142	1350	0802
113.	-2299	8231	3017	-0486	-1785
114.	1258	4791	2838	0118	0752
115.	-1440	3909	2975	1314	2402
116.	0858	3959	3246	1030	0594
117.	0819	3601	3799	1647	0227
118.	-0796	3803	5714	1057	2100
119.	-0528	3830	5924	1326	1892
120.	-0780	3432	5683	1081	2006
121.	-0472	2663	4587	0743	2153
122.	-1087	3100	6382	3288	1023
123.	-0888	3110	6483	3331	0938
124.	-1410	3926	6703	1010	0262
125.	-1116	3124	6651	0866	1285
126.	-0892	3571	6196	0953	0933
127.	-1628	5197	4378	0311	-0486
128.	0871	0864	2264	-1054	2123
129.	-0281	3539	4895	1376	-0711
130.	1287	1319	2958	2088	-0251
131.	-0354	1648	4456	0023	0560

Factors

Item	I	II	III	IV	V
132.	-0379	2483	4899	0246	0309
133.	2816	1494	4508	2229	1498
134.	1807	0680	5614	0836	0562
135.	2545	1622	4151	1645	0626
136.	2705	1905	4926	0486	0949
137.	1269	1965	7243	2709	-0177
138.	0758	1951	7250	2673	-0295
139.	1686	1135	5821	2454	-0268
140.	0402	2386	5456	0815	-0216
141.	-0340	1652	5888	1864	0200
142.	-0753	3535	4434	-0126	-1301
143.	0883	1199	4024	0515	0445
144.	-0221	2507	6600	1661	-0435
145.	0519	1411	3594	2288	-1543
146.	0738	2156	4949	0937	-0650
147.	1395	0733	6284	0415	0406
148.	1395	1239	6970	1020	0479
149.	-0296	2134	5954	1778	-0171
150.	0307	2224	6089	1264	0618
151.	1539	1530	5564	0992	0706
152.	1362	1094	5309	-0525	-0298

Eigenvalues

Item	I	II	III	IV	V
	17.72	16.99	16.22	13.19	14.71

Note: Factor loadings are rounded to four decimal places; decimal points are omitted.

APPENDIX P

Five-Factor Solution for a Factor Analysis of IMPORTANCE Responses: Oblique Transformation Using Promax Rotation

	Factors				
Item	I	II	III	IV	V
1.	3081	-0044	1927	5740	1179
2.	3013	1276	1720	5976	1175
3.	3377	0955	3411	6362	2116
4.	2177	0039	4071	6769	3232
5.	1856	-0998	4639	5789	3658
6.	2675	0733	3658	6120	3047
7.	3087	0296	3570	6753	2615
8.	2619	0153	3037	6456	2663
9.	3169	0434	2922	6843	2879
10.	3773	1410	1391	5663	1027
11.	4023	2784	2171	3235	2799
12.	3234	1023	3010	5434	2247
13.	3236	1180	2735	6935	2404
14.	1964	0335	2997	4876	1266
15.	3285	-0303	4034	5297	1333
16.	1893	-0676	5257	6478	2561
17.	1772	0779	3464	5173	2197
18.	3987	5093	0758	1368	0762
19.	1158	2703	0433	0806	1275
20.	0843	-0950	3940	4074	2280
21.	2090	-0872	5109	3680	2813
22.	4405	1319	3506	4980	1842
23.	2168	-1472	5140	2124	3343
24.	1253	1584	4199	0744	2599
25.	0551	0939	2222	3700	-0243
26.	2419	1477	3582	3463	-0915
27.	0084	-0887	4801	3067	3426
28.	1416	0208	5459	2376	3185
29.	0573	1325	4427	4216	2630
30.	0590	-1428	6683	2450	4408
31.	1111	1758	4336	4788	1194
32.	1389	0200	6091	4116	2683
33.	0422	-1598	6725	2443	4183
34.	0824	0697	2067	3256	1827
35.	2955	1326	2929	4458	2753
36.	3253	2095	2833	5089	3188
37.	3073	1667	3163	5216	2473
38.	2398	0545	4361	4341	2577

Factors

Item	I	II	III	IV	V
39.	3660	3505	1367	2244	1670
40.	2575	2024	4148	3430	3081
41.	4180	0824	2910	6441	1326
42.	3530	0676	2917	5880	1297
43.	3108	1853	2860	6078	2226
44.	2945	1133	3020	6972	2648
45.	2593	0880	3275	6131	2316
46.	2417	-0485	5343	4838	2433
47.	1769	1669	3470	4664	2611
48.	1957	1923	3072	4534	2538
49.	3098	2280	4223	3257	3138
50.	2772	7785	-0918	0444	-1160
51.	3650	1934	4436	3954	2757
52.	5296	2675	2965	2434	2174
53.	4741	1585	3735	2082	4148
54.	5373	2448	3313	2195	2502
55.	5778	3348	2985	1875	2736
56.	5249	1770	2695	3895	3368
57.	7071	3539	2300	2397	2311
58.	6774	3383	3115	2491	2983
59.	6698	3221	3151	2528	2955
60.	7026	3582	2672	2321	2508
61.	6003	2309	3479	3085	1386
62.	7018	3182	2702	3245	2110
63.	3286	-0957	6890	4791	4168
64.	2556	-1198	7659	4323	4048
65.	1998	-1548	7683	3991	3836
66.	2519	-1327	7674	4564	3647
67.	1588	-1724	7918	3496	3532
68.	3834	-0249	7077	4033	3105
69.	4082	-0190	7457	4300	3596
70.	4220	-0356	7234	4111	3546
71.	3475	-0541	6730	3826	3472
72.	2729	0634	6402	3408	1314
73.	0811	-1716	7128	2559	1859
74.	1194	-1215	7406	2868	1937
75.	1018	-0544	7290	2743	2562
76.	1794	-0905	6832	3847	1172
77.	1050	-1804	7777	3228	3578
78.	1002	-1441	7665	3245	3969
79.	2606	-0506	4545	3856	7471
80.	3023	-0551	4815	4446	7431
81.	2349	-0792	4617	3480	8408
82.	3020	-0353	4032	3907	8659
83.	1455	-0548	4066	2289	8419
84.	1836	-0717	4061	2783	8716

	Factors				
Item	I	II	III	IV	V
85.	2955	-0197	4328	3916	8053
86.	3839	-0124	3738	4330	8068
87.	2718	1005	2174	1419	7394
88.	2575	0678	2826	1754	7132
89.	3451	0689	3695	2776	7648
90.	2587	1382	2647	0875	4243
91.	2843	8204	-1152	1292	-1503
92.	2904	7806	-1536	0257	-0554
93.	2152	5439	0553	2855	1647
94.	2944	8086	-0916	1318	-1403
95.	4162	8088	-0592	0258	0821
96.	4424	6745	-0111	1164	-0330
97.	3293	8751	-1847	0259	-1499
98.	3184	8098	-1243	-0479	-0689
99.	3599	8629	-2092	-0405	-0952
100.	----	----	----	----	----
101.	3592	8515	-1729	-0123	-0630
102.	4633	3304	2725	0664	2695
103.	3455	6798	1227	-0446	1134
104.	3404	6846	-0454	1874	-2140
105.	4124	6252	0204	1826	-1990
106.	4373	7339	0118	1353	-0884
107.	4916	6821	-0407	2614	0726
108.	3986	7632	-0618	1648	0441
109.	2864	7138	-0732	1647	0575
110.	3982	7094	-0417	2103	0939
111.	3379	7851	-1058	0233	0048
112.	4015	6880	-0437	0152	1030
113.	3506	8085	-1242	0774	0187
114.	3540	5863	1105	2745	1108
115.	3456	5375	1142	1509	1243
116.	4666	5243	0769	3345	1362
117.	5001	4230	0912	3904	1355
118.	7447	4095	1764	3211	1868
119.	7564	4033	1707	3340	1979
120.	7706	4005	1894	2753	1644
121.	6951	3608	2620	2793	1733
122.	7723	3640	1222	2973	2874
123.	7922	3570	1270	3003	2801
124.	7495	3978	0414	2457	1450
125.	7658	3221	1377	2904	1645
126.	7278	4398	0448	2716	1274
127.	6161	5763	0488	1384	1514
128.	3907	1207	2483	2976	0930
129.	7233	3301	1028	4368	1753
130.	5891	2293	0971	4809	1349

Factors

Item	I	II	III	IV	V
131.	6588	2549	1741	2838	1270
132.	6948	2976	1351	2611	1500
133.	5492	1656	1894	5335	1567
134.	7460	2574	2065	3289	1705
135.	5531	1942	1169	5009	1117
136.	5799	2100	1544	5437	1304
137.	7647	3279	0838	3454	2651
138.	7576	3217	1239	3397	2877
139.	7108	2274	1586	2983	3030
140.	6982	3490	1949	2520	2043
141.	7070	2770	1529	2188	2653
142.	6411	4708	0862	0840	1011
143.	6175	2692	2290	1871	1373
144.	7822	3576	1117	2465	1776
145.	5419	2061	0891	2949	2347
146.	6174	2034	1205	3541	1584
147.	7007	2511	1872	3669	1949
148.	7607	2665	1913	3490	1651
149.	5521	2599	0995	2467	1594
150.	6906	2921	1807	2804	1871
151.	6278	2581	2135	2800	1820
152.	6733	2263	1693	2868	0877

Eigenvalues

Item	I	II	III	IV	V
	29.79	19.64	19.84	20.56	14.46

Note: Factor loadings are rounded to four decimal places; decimal points are omitted.

INDEX

INDEX

ABOUT NBCC

The National Board for Certified Counselors (NBCC) was incorporated in 1982 as an independent not-for-profit organization whose primary purposes are to establish and monitor a national counselor certification program, to identify to professionals and the public those counselors who voluntarily have sought and obtained certification, and to maintain a register of those counselors. NBCC was initiated through the efforts of the American Counseling Association (ACA) in the area of professional counselor credentialing.

Since its inception in 1982, NBCC has moved rapidly to the forefront of the counselor credentialing movement, implementing five national counselor certification programs: National Certified Counselor, National Certified Career Counselor, National Certified Gerontological Counselor, National Certified School Counselor, and Certified Clinical Mental Health Counselor. NBCC also promotes and supports high standards for the counseling profession in state counselor licensure and counselor education program accreditation.

ABOUT THE WORK BEHAVIOR STUDY PROJECT COORDINATORS

Larry C. Loesch, Ph.D., NCC

Dr. Loesch is a professor in the University of Florida's Counselor Education Department. He has published widely in the professional literature of counseling, with special emphasis in testing and measurement. He began NBCC's examination and development program in 1981 and has served as examination and research consultant since. Dr. Loesch is a leader in professional counseling at the state and national levels.

Nicholas A. Vacc, Ed.D., NCC, CCMHC

Dr. Vacc is professor and department chair of the Counselor Education Department at the University of North Carolina, Greensboro. Dr. Vacc was an early consultant in NBCC's examination development program and also has managed the scoring services of NBCC for 10 years. He is a national leader in the professional counseling movement. His numerous publications include research and testing as topics of emphasis. As a gifted editor, Dr. Vacc contributes extensive time to NBCC and the profession.